Our American Century

★

Rock & Roll Generation

★

Teen Life in the 50s

By the Editors of Time-Life Books, Alexandria, Virginia

With a Foreword by Dick Clark

Contents

★

Foreword

After the rock and roll generation burst onto the scene, America was never the same again. The Fabulous '50s—the wonderful period that this book brings to life—is one of those times that belong to all ages, like the Roaring '20s. The '50s became fabulous when a major upheaval occurred: The world became youth conscious, and teenagers developed their own taste in movies, cars, fashion, music, and media. What's more, they had the money to indulge their taste and became an economic force to be reckoned with. Teenagers wrapped their arms around music created by other young people—rhythm and blues and country performers. Rock and roll was born. Kids listened to their favorite disc jockeys playing this revolutionary new music on the radio and flocked to concerts. They watched black and white kids dance on the same dance floor without incident, right there on national television, on *American Bandstand*. It was still a local show in Philadelphia when I started hosting it in 1956, just a year after mainstream America went crazy over rock and roll. America's youth music eventually became one of our important international exports—from England to Japan, kids all around the world went crazy over rock and roll, too.

The new music succeeded in offending parents, religious leaders, musical old-timers, and politicians just as much as it excited the younger generation. The politicos tried to nip rock and roll in the bud. In their effort to grab headlines and votes, they flogged the music of the day. Fortunately, they failed to stamp it out. Some careers were ruined, but the music itself thrived, gaining popularity, stature, and even critical acclaim.

It's been my good fortune to be involved with rock and roll for four decades. The beat of the Fabulous '50s goes on.

Dancers swirl around Dick Clark in the American Bandstand studio. The show was a five-days-a-week, coast-to-coast teen institution.

Ecstatic Elvis fans let loose a chorus of screams during an April 1956 concert in Amarillo, Texas. The singer's closing number, "Blue Suede Shoes," brought down the house.

Swept away by his own performance during a 1958 photo session, aspiring rock and roller Tony Conn drops to the stage without missing a beat.

*Teens rock around a suburban Los Angeles
supermarket parking lot during a 1955
event featuring a local disc jockey.*

Bathed in the glow of a Wurlitzer jukebox, Chicago high schoolers ponder one of life's big decisions: choosing the right song.

The Roots
of Rock and Roll

One spring day in 1951 a Cleveland disc jockey named Alan Freed had one of those offhand conversations with a drinking buddy that shape history. His friend, Leo Mintz, ran the Record Rendez-vous, one of the city's largest record stores. The shop, which catered primarily to the city's black population, stocked a lot of what was then known in the industry as race music—rhythm and blues. To his surprise, he told Freed, hordes of white teenagers had begun coming in to buy rhythm and blues. They were even dancing in the aisles of the shop. "The beat is so strong," Mintz said, "that anyone can dance to it without a lesson."

This turn of events had given Mintz an idea for both boosting his own profits and promoting Freed's career. He already had helped Freed obtain his position as host of a classical music program on radio station WJW. Now, Mintz said, if Freed would persuade the station to replace the classical program with rhythm and blues, he would pay for the show by buying commercials for his record store. The proposal intrigued Freed, but he hesitated. The white-oriented stations that dared to play black music in those days were few and far between. It was the province of black stations that broadcast programs with such names as "Tan Town Jamboree" and "Sepia Swing Club." Rhythm and blues, Freed feared, was simply too raw and earthy for a large radio audience.

Nevertheless, Freed, an ambitious 29-year-old with a combative streak, smelled opportunity. Maybe Leo Mintz's new customers signaled that many more white teenagers were primed for some high-energy, high-hormone dance music: The top record on the pop charts that year was Patti Page's slow, mournful "Tennessee Waltz"—not the kind of music to make anybody dance in the aisles.

A capacity crowd of 10,000 people packs the Cleveland Arena to listen and dance to live music at Alan Freed's first concert, the Moondog Coronation Ball, in 1952.

U.S. Marines in Korea pass the bodies of comrades killed in an ambush by North Korean troops in December 1950. Over 33,000 Americans lost their lives in the three-year war.

Senator Joseph McCarthy's rampage against alleged Communists in and out of government climaxed in the 1954 Army-McCarthy hearings, which aired his charges against the military.

With his boss's permission, Freed's regular radio show was soon blaring out rhythm and blues at the end of the show, after the Bach and Beethoven. So many requests flooded in from teenagers in the white suburbs as well as from blacks that he launched a late-night show devoted entirely to rhythm and blues. He spun records featuring such performers as the Dominoes, Joe Turner, Ivory Joe Hunter, Ruth Brown, and Wynonie Harris. One of his listeners, Shirley Hayes, who was 18 and lived on the east side of Cleveland, later recalled that teenagers would hear this music playing through an open window and start dancing in the street.

Freed really got into the spirit of the sound. He called himself Moondog—a creature of the night baying in the darkness. He yipped and howled over the lively saxophone solo that was his opening theme song. He sipped Scotch, maintained a manic patter between records in his raspy voice, and backed up the beat of the music by banging on a thick Cleveland telephone book with a palm that got so raw he had to wear a golf glove.

Freed began to promote rhythm and blues outside the studio. Live performances of rhythm and blues artists were drawing big audiences, so Freed, hoping to capitalize on their success, put on his first show, the notorious Moondog Coronation Ball of March 21, 1952. This event, at which he intended to be crowned king, was scheduled for the Cleveland Arena, which had 10,000 seats. More than twice that many teenagers showed up, and the event had to be called off when thousands without tickets crashed the gates, touching off what may have been the major teen riot of the '50s. The well-publicized turmoil didn't hurt Freed professionally; in fact, he became known nationally as an entrepreneur of entertainment for the new teen market.

Freed came up with a special name for the music he was spinning on WJW. Perhaps to mask the fact that rhythm and blues was so closely identified with the black community and to make it more acceptable to white listeners, he started referring to the music as rock and roll. What Freed certainly knew but few whites were aware of at the time was that the term was widely used in black music as a euphemism for sex.

As rock and roll evolved its own special sound—a rich amalgam of both black and white traditions—it came to serve as the rallying cry for a new generation of young Americans. Adolescence for the first time became a separate subculture. Teens declared independence from their parents and adopted their own clothing, entertainment, idols, and even slang. Above all, they asserted themselves through a music so distinctly theirs that it defined an entire emerging generation.

A Context of Contrasts: The rock and roll generation sprang into being in a decade marked by contradictions: a perilous Cold War between the United States and the Soviet Union, political and social conformity, and unparalleled prosperity. While the kids of Cleveland were tuning in Alan Freed's lively show during the early '50s, young Americans still in their teens were soldiering halfway around the world in the divided little country of Korea. They were there to put out a major flareup in the Cold War that began when Communist North Korea invaded South Korea in 1950. The experience of the young soldiers was new: For the first time in U.S. history, black and white boys were fighting—and dying—side by side in fully integrated combat units.

Even after the Korean fighting ended in a frustrating stalemate in 1953, the Cold War cast a dark shadow over the decade. Development by both nations of hydrogen bombs that dwarfed in killing power the atomic devices dropped on Hiroshima and Nagasaki near the end of World War II raised the specter of mutual annihilation. The advance of Communism abroad bred further anxieties at home and gave rise to U.S. Senator Joseph McCarthy's crusade against purported subversives in government.

In contrast to this somber backdrop of international tension, suspicion, and mistrust was a widespread feeling of optimism. The majority of Americans had never had it so good economically. President Dwight D. Eisenhower, the former World War II general elected in 1952, presided over eight years of unprecedented prosperity. The backed-up demand for consumer goods—created by the war that the grandfatherly Ike helped win—generated an economic

Large suburban housing developments like Levittown in Long Island, New York (above), met the needs of the United States' burgeoning postwar population.

President Eisenhower and Vice President Nixon raise a victory salute after winning a second term in 1956. Widespread prosperity and Ike's winning personality convinced even longtime Democrats to vote Republican.

Martin Luther King Jr. and Ralph D. Abernathy ride in the front of the first bus to be desegregated in Montgomery, Alabama, in December 1956. The two ministers led the successful 381-day boycott of the city's transit system by black residents.

By 1956 Americans owned 42 million television sets, and family comedies like Father Knows Best (below) were favorite viewing fare.

boom. By the millions, Americans snapped up television sets and the things advertised on their little black-and-white screens: refrigerators, washing machines, and automobiles with tail fins so large they looked poised for takeoff. Housing developments like Long Island's Levittown—mass-produced and look-alike but made affordable by government-backed loans—fulfilled for millions the American dream of owning their own home.

Growing Up Smart: Most of those new homes were filling up with children as a result of the postwar baby boom. Never had Americans focused so much attention on education. School enrollment during the decade jumped by 30 percent, and new classrooms could not be constructed quickly enough to meet the need. What happened in the classroom came under increasing criticism. The prevalent ideas of progressive education fostered by the American philosopher John Dewey, with their emphasis on "life adjustment" and learning by doing, were attacked as too permissive. Books with titles such as *Why Johnny Can't Read* became bestsellers.

These concerns escalated after the Soviet Union orbited the first man-made satellite, Sputnik, in 1957. The Communists had leapfrogged U.S. technology, it was alleged, because of the failure of American schools to teach science and mathematics adequately. *Life* magazine, in its five-part series entitled "Crisis in Education," depicted the contrasting lives of two typical 16-year-old high-school students—Stephen Lapekas of Chicago and Alexei Kutzkov of Moscow. Young Lapekas came out happier, *Life* reported, but his Russian counterpart was academically "two years ahead of Stephen." One result of all the publicity was congressional passage in 1958 of the most significant legislation mandating federal aid to education in nearly a century.

A profounder crisis in American education took place in thousands of racially segregated southern school districts. In 1954, the U.S. Supreme Court ruled against the old "separate but equal" doctrine. "Separate educational facilities," wrote Chief Justice Earl Warren, "are inherently unequal." To enforce this new law of the land, President Eisenhower had to send elite troops from the 101st Airborne Division to Little Rock, Arkansas, in 1957. Backed by federal bayonets, nine intrepid black teenagers integrated Central High School, defying the threats of white fellow students as well as the protests of white crowds outside the school.

The Roots of Rock: Though generally excluded from '50s prosperity—the battle for equal rights was just beginning—black Americans possessed a priceless musical heritage. It included the church gospel-singing tradition that had grown out of the complex rhythms and call-and-response vocal rituals brought from Africa. Another part of the tradition was the blues, blending work chants with the joys and sorrows of life in the South. Finally, there was 20th-century jazz, from ragtime to the sophisticated swing of composers and musicians like Duke Ellington and Lionel Hampton. These disparate elements came together as rhythm and

Angry whites confront black teenagers attempting to integrate a school in North Little Rock, Arkansas, in 1957. The 1954 Supreme Court ruling that struck down the "separate but equal" doctrine met stiff resistance in the South.

blues during the late '40s and early '50s. Fused with a pulsating beat, they provided the foundation for rock and roll. Rhythm and blues evolved from the black music that was transplanted from the South during the great migration to northern cities. A guitar-playing native of the Mississippi Delta named McKinley Morganfield took a gritty form of the blues to Chicago under the stage name Muddy Waters. Singer and saxophonist Louis Jordan from Arkansas and his Tympany Five played a peppy version known as jump music, with sassy lyrics, comic verve, and a boogie-woogie beat accentuated by electronic amplifiers. Boosting the sound electronically allowed the little bands to be heard in the noisy urban bars where they played. It also enabled bluesmen to improvise with startling re-

The Russian satellite Sputnik zooms past a startled Uncle Sam in this 1957 cartoon. Americans were alarmed by this evidence of the advanced state of Russian technology.

Arthur "Big Boy" Crudup

Louis Jordan

Aaron "T-Bone" Walker

Among the black rhythm and blues stars shown above and on the opposite page is Willie Mae "Big Mama" Thornton, who recorded "Hound Dog" in 1953, three years before Elvis Presley made it a rock and roll hit.

sults. Aaron "T-Bone" Walker from Dallas, a pioneer on the electric guitar, played so passionately that it was said he could make the instrument cry the blues and wail gospel.

White teenagers, accustomed to singers like Perry Como, Patti Page, Eddie Fisher, and Rosemary Clooney, were astonished when they heard such music. But even the big record companies were starting to experiment with novelty per-

Willie Mae "Big Mama" Thornton

formers. In 1952, a skinny, half-deaf white singer named Johnny Ray sold four million records with "The Little White Cloud That Cried" on one side and just plain "Cry" on the other. The lyrics were conventional enough, but not Ray's delivery. Nicknamed the Nabob of Sob, he squirmed, choked in agony, and fell to his knees weeping—histrionics not unlike those performed by later rockers. But Ray faded quickly as teenagers found in rhythm and blues the raw emotion and direct communication they had been seeking—whether they knew it or not.

The Hillbilly Factor: Precisely when and where rhythm and blues left off and rock began would become a subject of endless scholarly debate. "The blues had a baby," Muddy Waters sang, "and they called it rock and roll." But virtually from the beginning rock received a powerful injection from another southern musical tradition. So-called hillbilly music, or country and western in industry parlance, evolved from early folk music played and sung by rural whites in the South. Like rhythm and blues, it was considered fringe music. Similarly, its chief adherents—poor southern whites—lived on the margin of society like poor blacks.

Hillbilly owed much to the black tradition but had its own unique characteristics. These were best exemplified in the great performer Hank Williams. In a career cut short by death when he was only 29, Williams recorded such hits as "Jambalaya," "Hey, Good Lookin'," and "Your Cheatin' Heart." He sang with a nasal twang, *Billboard* noted, "in true backwoods fashion, with a tear in his voice."

It was no accident that one of the first groups widely labeled as

Hank Williams

rock and rollers, Bill Haley and His Comets, started out in hillbilly. Haley had even yodeled before his group borrowed the big beat from rhythm and blues for "Crazy Man, Crazy" in 1953 and then the wildly successful "Rock Around the Clock." Hillbilly repaid some of its debt to black music in the person of Chuck Berry, a St. Louis hairdresser. Berry, who in 1955 blended country with rhythm and blues in "Maybellene," crossed over to the mainstream pop charts and became the most influential black performer of early rock and roll.

Down in Memphis, a center of southern black music, Sam Phillips of little Sun Records was looking for someone who could combine both traditions. He had been recording such outstanding rhythm and bluesmen as B. B. King, but for commercial reasons Phillips hoped to find an energetic and entertaining singer who also happened to be white. Phillips found him in Elvis Presley, a 19-year-old truckdriver who wore pegged pants and a ducktail haircut with long sideburns. His role models were the movie renegades Marlon Brando and James Dean. He had learned to sing and play the guitar by imitating the hillbilly music on the radio and the gospel singing he heard in church. He also had frequented the blues bars of Beale Street and the black roadhouses of his native Mississippi and knew a song written and performed by a bluesman named Arthur "Big Boy" Crudup. Elvis recorded "That's All Right" for Sam Phillips's Sun label on July 5, 1954, began shaking his hips soon thereafter, and launched a cultural revolution.

B. B. King

Ruth Brown

Big Joe Turner

A Golden Age: With Elvis lighting the fuse with his captivating hybrid of hillbilly, rhythm and blues, and something more, rock and roll exploded into the national consciousness. In 1957, a year after Elvis's television debut, rock accounted for fully two-thirds of the 60 best-selling records in the United States. By echoing the vitality and feeling of separateness that animated adolescence, it became the bedrock of the new teenage nation. Rock was written and performed by young people and focused on what was important to them. It celebrated teenage style ("Blue

The honky-tonk sound of Hank Williams (above, top) was absorbed by Elvis Presley, Bill Haley, and other early rock and rollers. The country star's onstage hip wiggling was also carried on by his admirers.

The Clovers

The Dominoes

The Orioles

Formed in the 1940s, the Orioles (bottom) gained white fans with their 1953 song "Crying in the Chapel." Their popularity among whites smoothed the way for other black groups like the Dominoes and the Clovers.

Suede Shoes"), slang ("Be-Bop-a-Lula"), love ("Earth Angel"), and freedom from parental control ("Yakety Yak"). Recalling the nights when he lay on his bed listening to rock on the radio, an early convert to the new music wrote, "To a twelve- or thirteen-year-old, it was a world of unbearable sexuality and celebration: a world of citizens under sixteen, in a constant state of joy or sweet sorrow."

The architects of that world were the disc jockeys as well as the performers. During the mid '50s, which would later be referred to nostalgically as rock's golden age, they spun a special verbal mystique while spinning the records. Teenagers looked upon them as authority figures who reaffirmed their independence and guided them through the new musical realm. Most of the estimated 3,500 disc jockeys in the United States were white, though some employed black coaches to help them sound more authentic in dispensing their jive talk. The greatest of them all, the gravel-voiced Alan Freed, needed no such instruction. After christening the new music in Cleveland, in 1954 Freed moved to New York's WINS, where he established himself as the nation's leading promoter of rock. Mercenary as well as visionary, he hosted a network radio show, appeared in five rock movies, sponsored tumultuous live concert tours that sometimes erupted in violence, and—before Elvis ascended the throne—proclaimed himself the king of rock and roll.

Teens as Consumers: As rock soared to the top of the charts, the major record companies moved in. They took over a market that had been made up primarily of small independent producers like Sam Phillips's Sun Records in Memphis. Hoping to broaden the music's appeal and boost sales, they produced new versions of songs already recorded on the little rhythm and blues labels. These so-called covers featured white performers such as the Crew-Cuts, a Canadian group whose version of "Sh-Boom" outsold the highly successful original by the black Chords. White covers typically smoothed

Faye Adams, famed for her recording of "Shake a Hand," a song about racial harmony.

out the musical arrangement and sanitized lyrics deemed too sexy for a young audience. Thus, Etta James's risqué "Roll With Me Henry" became the toned-down white cover version "Dance With Me Henry." In addition to cleaning up the words, the major labels frequently substituted white performers such as Pat Boone, whose public image was impeccably wholesome. Many disc jockeys played covers because they thought them more suitable for white listeners. One notable exception was Alan Freed, who stuck stubbornly to the original versions.

Rock became big business, and the teen culture that coalesced around it turned into a booming segment of the consumer economy. And it kept growing: The U.S. teen population reached 13 million in 1956. Bigger allowances and the easy availability of part-time jobs enabled young people to share in the general prosperity and to help fuel it *(pages 98-109)*. A teenager could buy a state-of-the-art transistor radio for $25. An Elvis Presley portable record player, which handled a stack of the new compact 45-rpm discs, sold for $47.95—$1 down and $1 a week. Thanks largely to rock and its young consumers, record sales more than tripled during the '50s. By the end of the decade, the teenage market for all consumer goods amounted to no less than $10 billion.

LaVern Baker

Though the big-time commercialization of rock tamed it somewhat, the new music caused consternation in much of the adult world. Critics blamed rock for societal ills ranging from juvenile delinquency to loosened sexual standards. According to one vigorous indictment, rock was "the most brutal, ugly, degenerate, vicious form of expression it has been my displeasure to hear. It fosters almost totally negative and destructive reactions in young people. It smells phony and false. It is sung, played and written for the most part by cretinous goons."

The speaker was the veteran singer Frank Sinatra, the same crooner who had so mesmerized bobbysoxers during the '40s. In fact, many of the young women who had worried their parents by shrieking and swooning over Sinatra were now the mothers who fretted about the behavior of their rock-and-roll-generation offspring.

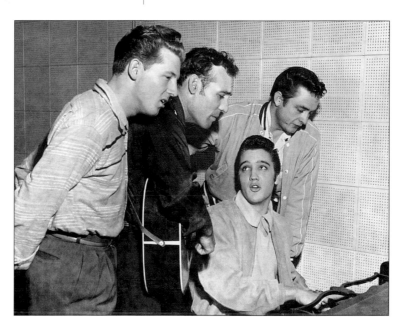

Jerry Lee Lewis, Carl Perkins, Elvis Presley, Johnny Cash

LaVern Baker (above, top) recorded on the Atlantic label, while at various times Sun Records boasted Jerry Lee Lewis, Carl Perkins, Elvis Presley, and Johnny Cash, shown left to right in a 1956 photo.

The Power of the Beat

★

ROCK AND ROLL TAKES OFF

The new music burst upon America with all the rowdy exuberance of Little Richard swinging his leg up on the piano. And if watching and listening from the audience was exciting, being onstage was beyond compare. "That piano was talkin' and the drums was walkin', " said Little Richard. "It made my big toe shoot up in my boot." The words of rock and roll songs were so charged with sexual innuendo that critics called them "leer-ics." The high decibel level of electric guitars *(inset)* made the new music even hotter. Above all, though, it was the beat that distinguished rock and roll—a syncopated "backbeat," as the musicians called it, that irresistibly got teens up and dancing. "It's got a backbeat, you can't lose it," sang Chuck Berry in his 1957 hit "Rock and Roll Music." Fats Domino's song "The Big Beat" made just the same point.

1957 Fender Stratocaster

Heavy and insistent, the beat possessed such power that, borrowed as it was from black music, it even began to subvert rigid old racial barriers. At concerts, white teenagers listened and danced to it in the company of their black counterparts. Chuck Berry remembered his amazement when he saw audiences starting to integrate: "Salt and pepper all mixed together, and we'd say, 'Well, look what's happening.' "

YOU ROCK AND I'LL ROLL

Little Richard is all energy in the 1957 movie Mr. Rock and Roll. The film also featured Chuck Berry, LaVern Baker, Clyde McPhatter, the Moonglows, Frankie Lymon and the Teenagers, and disc jockey Alan Freed.

Rock's National Anthem

Bill Haley was the least likely of the early rockers. A yodeler and small-town Pennsylvania disc jockey, he had a moon-faced grin, a spit curl that looped over his forehead, and a pickup band known as the Saddlemen, who wore cowboy boots and played country and western. Then Haley renamed his group the Comets and changed their sound. One of their first new songs was "Rock Around the Clock." A catchy blend of rhythm and blues and country that came to be called rockabilly, it was featured in the 1955 film *Blackboard Jungle* and promptly shot to the top of the charts.

Both the song and the film's story of rebellious youth resonated with the new teen culture. In Buffalo, young motorists responded predictably when a disc jockey climbed atop a billboard and urged them to honk their horns if they wanted to hear "Rock Around the Clock": They honked and honked for this battle cry of their new freedom.

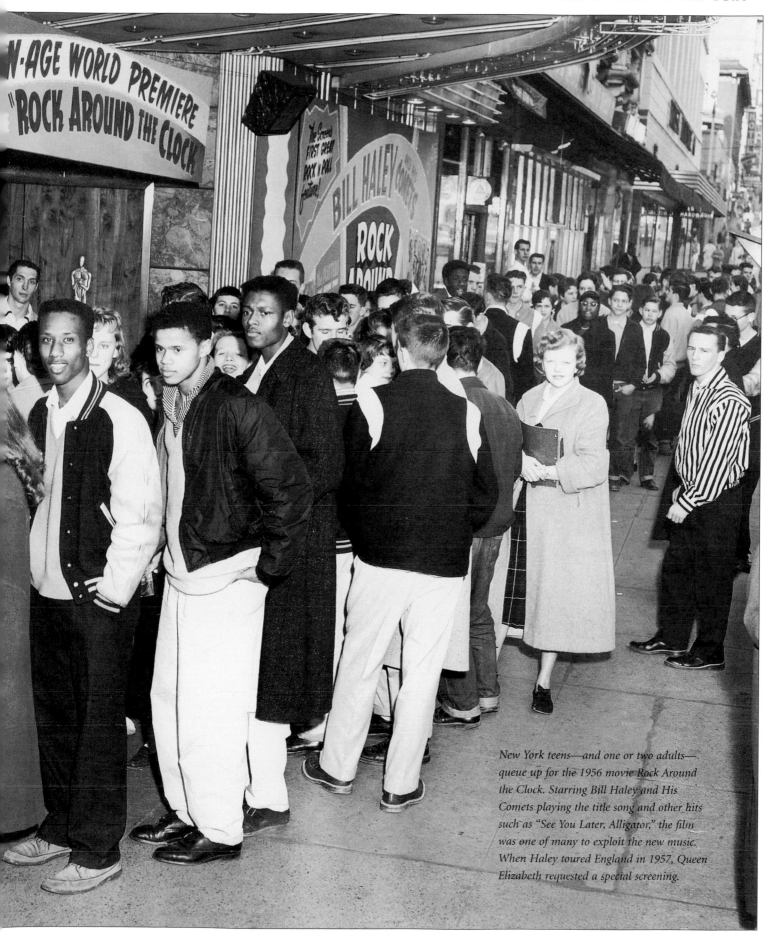

New York teens—and one or two adults—
queue up for the 1956 movie Rock Around
the Clock. Starring Bill Haley and His
Comets playing the title song and other hits
such as "See You Later, Alligator," the film
was one of many to exploit the new music.
When Haley toured England in 1957, Queen
Elizabeth requested a special screening.

Bill Haley's Comets "get down"—two of them literally—during a concert. The plaid jackets are holdovers from the group's days as a country and western band.

The Poet Laureate

In 1955 a handsome 29-year-old St. Louis hairdresser and part-time blues guitarist made one last stab at stardom. Chuck Berry, who already had been turned down by three record companies, made a crude demonstration tape and sent it to Chess Records, a small Chicago rhythm and blues label.

"Hail, hail, rock and roll. Deliver me from the days of old."

Chuck Berry, "School Day," 1957

This time one song practically leaped from the tape. Berry had taken the country tune "Ida Red," grafted onto it what he called his "boogie beat," and enlivened the whole with sly lyrics and scorching guitar riffs. Chess released the piece as a single entitled "Maybellene"—supposedly the name of a cow in Berry's old third-grade reader. Its story of girls and fast cars appealed directly to teenagers. Follow-up hits such as "Roll Over Beethoven," "Brown-Eyed

Plugging his 1957 album After School Session, Berry poses with fans in Waco, Texas.

Handsome Man," "School Day," "Rock and Roll Music," "Sweet Little Sixteen," "Johnny B. Goode," and "Memphis, Tennessee" also celebrated teendom with wit and honesty. Added to this, Berry's stage antics—including his famous duck walk—sent his popularity skyrocketing.

Virtually alone among rock and roll's pioneers, Berry composed his own music and wrote his own lyrics. He won praise from his fellow musicians as "the poet laureate of rock." And there would soon be imitators aplenty on both sides of the ocean, including an entranced young listener in Liverpool named John Lennon.

Berry performs his signature duck walk. According to legend, he devised this show-stopper to hide the wrinkles in a new seersucker suit. He actually perfected it as a boy when he would strut around under the kitchen table to amuse his family.

He said his songs were not "about me but about the people listening."

"A-wop-bop-a-loo-bop-a-wop-bam-boom."

Little Richard, "Tutti-Frutti," 1955

Three Kings of the Keyboard

Although the electric guitar was the very epitome of rock and roll, three of rock's biggest early stars made their mark with an instrument normally associated with more refined forms of music—the piano. The keyboard pounding of Little Richard—born Richard Wayne Penniman in Macon, Georgia—was the perfect accompaniment for his chaotic vocals. The former child gospel singer moaned, wailed, and screamed such teen favorites as "Tutti-Frutti" and "Long Tall Sally." He gave away the rights to "Tutti" in 1955 for only $50 but still earned enough to carry around a trunkload of cash in his car and let needy friends help themselves.

When Jerry Lee Lewis went on his first concert tour after recording "Crazy Arms," he was so shy that a colleague advised him, "Make a fuss!" Lewis started singing atop the piano and kicking the bench around. Once, in an attempt to upstage Chuck Berry, he even poured lighter fluid on the lid and set it aflame while pounding out his trademark "Great Balls of Fire."

Antoine "Fats" Domino actually sat at the piano to perform such tunes as "Blueberry Hill" and "Ain't That a Shame" in a mellow New Orleans blues mode. However sedentary, Fats could still stir an audience. He attributed a riot at one of his concerts to "the beat and the booze."

This publicity photo captures the essence of Little Richard's wide-open personality. Always the showman, he cultivated a bizarre public image by wearing mascara and a six-inch pompadour.

HERE'S LITTLE RICHARD

Belting out a song atop his piano (left) or pounding on a cartoon keyboard (above), Jerry Lee Lewis is a hair-flopping ball of fire.

Debonair in one of his more than 50 tan silk suits, Fats Domino croons to the microphone while fixing an eye on his audience.

The portable player at left, featuring a photo of Elvis Presley, accommodated 45-rpm records with an adapter at the base of its spindle. Lively images on the record sleeves shown here, all favorites during the 1950s, include many of familiar performers.

> ## "The theater is jammed with adolescents from the 9 a.m. curtain to closing, and it rings and shrieks like the jungle-bird house at the zoo."
>
> *Time* magazine, 1956

An integrated audience reacts with wild enthusiasm to Freed's Easter show at the Paramount in Brooklyn in 1955. Rock revues crisscrossed the country during the '50s; the poster at right is for a star-packed Kansas show.

Rock on the Road

To promote their latest releases, performers toured the nation presenting live concerts. Chuck Berry and other top stars often spent more than 300 days a year on the road. In the South they sometimes faced audiences in which black and white teens were separated by chicken-wire fencing to satisfy segregation laws. Sniffing the potential for big profits, promoters soon began assembling all-star casts for coast-to-coast tours stopping at major cities. Entrepreneurs such as Alan Freed and Irving Feld vied with one another to sign up the biggest names. Performers jostled for top billing, and teens competed for seats, lining up before dawn to get tickets and the opportunity, as one put it, "to scream all you like." Audiences frequently surrendered to such a frenzy of shrieking, dancing, and even rioting that the *New York Times* likened a rock concert to "having an aisle seat for the San Francisco earthquake."

TUESDAY NITE NOV. 5

ADVANCE ADMISSION $2.00--AT DOOR $2.50

CKETS ON SALE AT WALGREEN'S DRUG STORE, HOURS 8:00 P. M. to 12

er Attractions present ★ IN PERSON

HE BIGGEST *SHOW OF STARS* FOR '57

Fats Domino and his ORCHESTRA

LaVern "JIM DANDY" BAKER

Frankie LYMON "GOODY GOODY"

Clyde McPhatter "LONG, LONELY NIGHTS"

"THAT'LL BE THE DAY" **THE CRICKETS**

CHUCK BERRY "SCHOOLDAYS"

EVERLY BROS. "BYE, BYE, LOVE"

Eddie **OCHRAN**

The DIAMONDS "ZIP ZIP"

The DRIFTERS

BUDDY KNOX "Party Doll"

"DIANA" **Paul Anka**

JIMMY BOWEN and the RHYTHM ORCHIDS

Plus PAUL WILLIAMS and his BIG ORCHESTRA

The Adults Fight Back

Director of the FBI J. Edgar Hoover labeled it "a corrupting influence." *Music Journal* called it "a menace to morals." A White Citizens' Council spokesman in Alabama, noting that it fostered racial integration, saw a "plot to mongrelize America." From all angles, the adult world launched attacks on the teenagers' new music. *Time* likened rock concerts to "Hitler mass meetings." A Columbia University psychiatrist, Joost Meerlo, drew a parallel to St. Vitus's dance, a bizarre form of hysteria characterized by uncontrollable writhing and jerking. The city of Boston even went so far as to ban rock concerts after several were marred by violent incidents.

Teenagers seemed a bit perplexed by the older generation's reaction. Echoing the plight of adolescents since time immemorial, an Arizona high-school student complained, "Man, I believe the older generation just doesn't want the younger generation to have any fun."

Bible in one hand and concert poster in the other, a Baptist preacher denounces rock and roll as a "new low in spiritual degeneracy." Headlines pressed the attack.

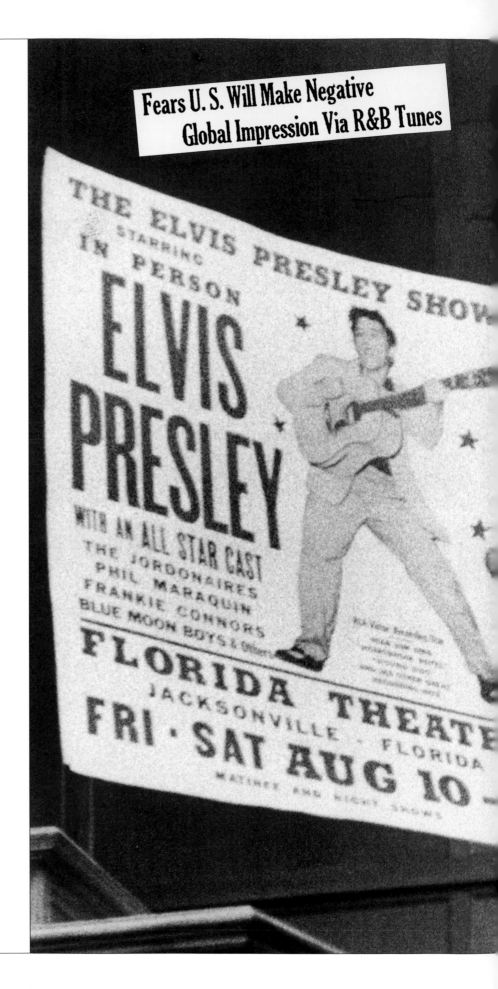

Fears U. S. Will Make Negative Global Impression Via R&B Tunes

Segregationist Wants
Ban on 'Rock and Roll'

Rock-and-Roll Called
'Communicable Disease'

EXPERTS PROPOSE
STUDY OF 'CRAZE'

Liken It to Medieval Lunacy,
'Contagious Dance Furies'
and Bite of Tarantula

A Pat Answer

Every parent worried about rock found the antidote to Elvis in singer Pat Boone—"the first teen-age idol that grandma can dig too," as one magazine put it. The great-great-great-great-grandson of Daniel Boone and a lay preacher in the Church of Christ, he didn't smoke, drink, curse, or swivel his pelvis. He was also a family man, happily married to his high-school sweetheart and the father of four.

"Great cooga mooga!"

Pat Boone's pet expression

Boone recorded both old-fashioned ballads and bland cover versions of such rock hits as "Tutti-Frutti" and "Ain't That a Shame." His repertoire of moves consisted of nothing more outrageous than foot tapping and finger snapping. By the age of 24 he had starred in three films, sold 20 million records, hosted his own network TV show, graduated from Columbia University magna cum laude, and written a best-selling book of advice for his fans.

Projecting an image as spotless as his suit, Pat Boone models for a clothing advertisement that appeared in Life magazine. The admiring director of one of his movies thought the singer-turned-Hollywood star was "too good to be true."

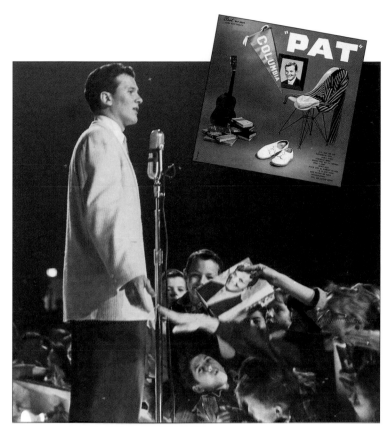

Displaying an upright posture rare among rock stars, Boone enraptures a Montgomery, Alabama, audience in 1957. His trademark white bucks, shown with other Boone artifacts on the album cover at top, were reassuringly mainstream.

Devoted to wife Shirley and daughters Debbie, Cherry, Lindy, and baby Laury, Boone refused to kiss any woman but his spouse. The scene at right with Shirley Jones from their 1957 film April Love was about as close as he came.

Boonerisms

Below are samples of advice from the singer's book, the number two nonfiction bestseller of 1958.

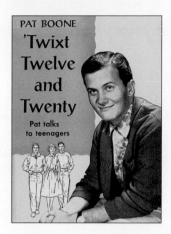

On spirituality
Your whole future, your whole sense of identity, belonging and purpose may never become clear unless you start with your spiritual growth.

On finances
Work and money are the freedom twins. Money in the bank means greater freedom of mind and action and we don't get financial security without working for it.

On going steady
I would say it's a wise guy and gal who are willing to let there be some spaces in their togetherness.

On kissing
It's not a game. Believe me! A kiss is a beautiful expression of love—real love. Kissing for fun is like playing with a beautiful candle in a roomful of dynamite.

Sweet Harmony From the Streets

A brand of rock and roll with a sound all its own first echoed off the brownstones and blacktop of urban neighborhoods around the nation. In groups of four or five, black teenagers, both male and female, would gather on street corners to harmonize sweet, innocent lyrics of love. The style was remarkably consistent: a soaring soprano or falsetto line over deeper voices, with musical bridges that were spoken, not sung. Unaccompanied by instruments, the singers improvised the sound of drums by snapping their fingers and the rhythm of the bass by repeating nonsense syllables—from which came a name for this music: doo-wop.

The Coasters

LIttle Anthony and the Imperials

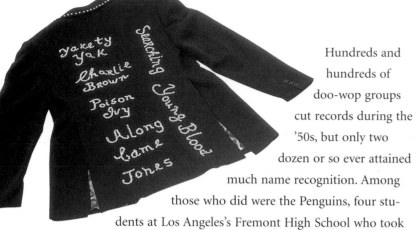

Hundreds and hundreds of doo-wop groups cut records during the '50s, but only two dozen or so ever attained much name recognition. Among those who did were the Penguins, four students at Los Angeles's Fremont High School who took their name from the trademark of Kool cigarettes. The Penguins' recording of "Earth Angel" became an all-time favorite. Another well-known group, the Coasters—so named because they came from the West Coast—actually started out as the Robins, following the trend of choosing bird names. The Coasters' specialty was amusing novelty numbers, whose names lead tenor Carl Gardner had emblazoned on the back of his tuxedo jacket in gold sequins *(above)*.

Names That Soar and Roar

In naming their groups, doo-wop singers gravitated toward certain categories. Birds and automobiles were especially popular.

Birds	Cars
Cardinals	Belairs
Crows	Bonnevilles
Eagles	Cadillacs
Flamingos	Continentals
Jayhawks	Edsels
Night Owls	Fleetwoods
Peacocks	Impalas
Penguins	Montereys
Quails	Ramblers
Wrens	Thunderbirds

The Platters

Frankie Lymon and the Teenagers

Teen Idols by Formula

Entrepreneurs searching for new rockers to promote made a happy discovery: A pretty-boy face that appealed to the fast-growing female audience could be the key to success. They could let the music take care of itself. With the help of Dick Clark's *American Bandstand (pages 56-59)*, Bob Marcucci, president of Philadelphia's Chancellor Records, turned two local boys into teen idols. He spotted 14-year-old Fabian—Fabiano Forte —sitting on the steps outside his home. Frankie Avalon, a trumpet-playing prodigy who was just learning to be a singer, was Marcucci's other find.

Unlike Fabian and Frankie, Ricky Nelson was already in the public eye thanks to his family's weekly TV show, *The Adventures of Ozzie and Harriet.* At 16, to impress a girlfriend infatuated with Elvis, he recorded the Fats Domino hit "I'm Walkin' " and performed it on the family show. Paired with "A Teenager's Romance," the song sold 60,000 copies in the first three days; total sales exceeded one million. A long string of top-10 hits followed. To the critics' amazement, Nelson, who'd never been interested in singing before, turned out to be more than just a pretty face.

With his teen sex appeal, Fabian (above) overcame charges that "he couldn't sing a note" to sell one million copies of his 1959 single "Tiger."

The cover of a 1958 Ricky Nelson album offered fans another look at those irresistible eyes. Songs included "Poor Little Fool."

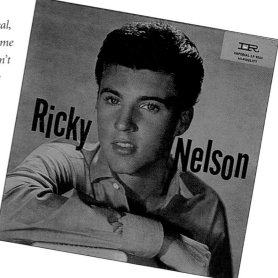

Just a touch of Frankie Avalon's hand elicits high-voltage emotion from a fan who waited all day in the rain to see his concert.

New Wave, Novel Styles

In 1957, two new and distinctly different acts added to the range of rock music. The sweet-singing Everly Brothers, brought up in a country music family, became rock stars almost by accident when they recorded "Bye Bye Love." A mix of folk harmony and the big beat, the song had been rejected by 30 other acts. Ten days after the Everlys made their recording it hit the pop charts, and the handsome brothers were well on the way to becoming teen idols. A less likely-looking star was Buddy Holly, who broke through that same year with "That'll Be the Day," a playful account of a strained romance. A lean Texan from Lubbock, Holly had played in country acts throughout high school. Then, in 1955, Elvis came to Lubbock, and Holly was hired to open the show. Stunned by Presley's performance, he committed himself to rock and roll.

The Everly Brothers

Outfitted identically right down to the guitar strap, Phil (near right) and Don brought to rock their own tradition of country harmony, with tightly woven tenor voices atop a steady beat. Beginning with "Bye Bye Love" and "Wake Up Little Susie," they averaged a top-10 hit every four months for three years. Their following was so rapturous that they had to keep extra clothes on hand to replace the ones fans ripped apart.

Buddy Holly

Buddy Holly wrote most of his songs himself, including "Peggy Sue" and "Fade Away," two of several chartbusters he recorded with the Crickets. Holly hooked audiences with an unusual vocal delivery featuring a kind of hiccup and gliding runs from falsetto to deep bass. Unlike other rock stars with poor vision, he didn't bat an eye about wearing his glasses onstage.

Acoustic guitar with leather cover hand-tooled by Holly

An End to Innocence

Late in the decade, rock suffered a crisis so severe that a record executive likened it to "a coma, almost." It began in 1957 when Little Richard forsook the new music and enrolled in a Bible college. In March 1958, Elvis was drafted into the U.S. Army. A few months later, the Louisiana fireball Jerry Lee Lewis fell into disgrace after marrying his 13-year-old cousin *(opposite)*.

The bad news accelerated in 1959. One of rock and roll's greatest talents, Buddy Holly, was killed along with two other singers when their small plane crashed in Iowa. Then Chuck Berry fell afoul of the law on a tour of the Southwest. He took a 14-year-old girl back to work in his St. Louis nightclub, triggering a legal battle that led to his two-year imprisonment for violating the Mann Act, which forbade transporting a minor across state lines for immoral purposes. The suspicion that the establishment was trying to stamp out rock seemed confirmed at the end of the decade when its greatest proselytizer, Alan Freed, was enmeshed in scandal. "Now they're trying to take our father away!" wailed a tearful teen disciple.

"The Day the Music Died"

Three of Buddy Holly's colleagues on the Winter Dance Party tour work the crowd in Kenosha, Wisconsin: 17-year-old Ritchie Valens (standing, far left) of "La Bamba" fame; Dion DiMucci (standing next to Valens), who sang with the Belmonts; and J. P. Richardson, "the Big Bopper," wearing the leopard-skin jacket. Ten days later, on February 3, 1959, a chartered plane carrying Holly, the Bopper, and Valens crashed near Clear Lake, Iowa, killing all three singers. For many teens the tragedy came to embody rock's loss of innocence.

The Wages of Spin

The practice of "payola"—payment by record companies to disc jockeys to play a new release—had been prevalent in radio for years. When congressional investigators focused on the practice late in 1959, they targeted rock and roll. Alan Freed, its leading promoter, who had foes as well as 2,000 fan clubs, became the scapegoat. After he refused to sign an affidavit denying he had accepted payola, New York's WABC fired him. He later was found guilty of commercial bribery and charged with income-tax evasion. Shunned by the industry he helped create, Freed died at age 43 of alcoholism.

New York Post

EXCLUSIVE By EARL WILSON

ALAN FREED TELLING ALL
Meets Payola Probers

Jerry Lee and Cousin Myra

At age 22 the flamboyant Jerry Lee Lewis already had been married twice, and U.S. newspapers didn't pay much attention when he took a third bride early in 1958. But while he was on tour in England that spring, he made the mistake of revealing some shocking information to reporters: His new wife, the former Myra Gayle Brown, was only 13 years old and his cousin to boot. Scandalized Britons booed him off the stage, and the newlyweds returned home in disgrace. His rock career, which was soaring at the time, went into a tailspin.

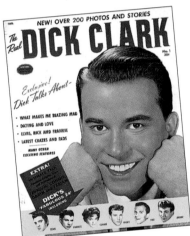

America's Most Popular Bandstand

In 1956, when Dick Clark was assigned to emcee a TV dance party on Philadelphia's WFIL, he had "only a foggy notion of what the kids, music and show were really about." He proved to be a quick study, however. A year later, his *American Bandstand* was a five-days-a-week feature on the ABC network, and teenagers all over the nation rushed home from school every afternoon to watch.

Clark spun the latest records while his 150 guests, mostly Philadelphia high-school students, staged a 90-minute dance-a-thon so wholesome that even mothers looked on with approval. By example, these TV teens taught their peers at home not only how to do the latest dance (nothing too sexy) but also how to behave (no smoking or gum chewing) and dress (jackets and ties for boys, proper dresses for girls). Some of the kids who appeared regularly—Carmen Jimenez, Bob Clayton, and Justine Carelli among others—even had their own fan clubs. The show was so popular that it transformed local balladeers Frankie Avalon and Fabian into nationwide sensations.

Clark soon became a powerful force in the music industry. By decade's end he held the copyrights to more than 160 songs and owned shares in more than 30 corporations, including record and music-publishing enterprises. Like practically everyone else in the business, he came under scrutiny in 1959 during the payola investigations. Though Clark vehemently denied taking payola, the issue of conflict of interest inevitably arose every time he played a record from one of his own labels. At ABC's prompting, he gave up all of his outside music holdings. Emerging from the scandal unscathed, Clark led *Bandstand* into the new decade and to new heights of popularity.

Dick Clark's fresh face and broad smile were virtual trademarks on every American Bandstand broadcast. He and the show's regular dancers were frequently the subject of feature stories in teen magazines (left).

His face contorted with excitement, a dancer moves to the beat on American Bandstand. Teens across the country watched the show to see the latest styles and dance steps.

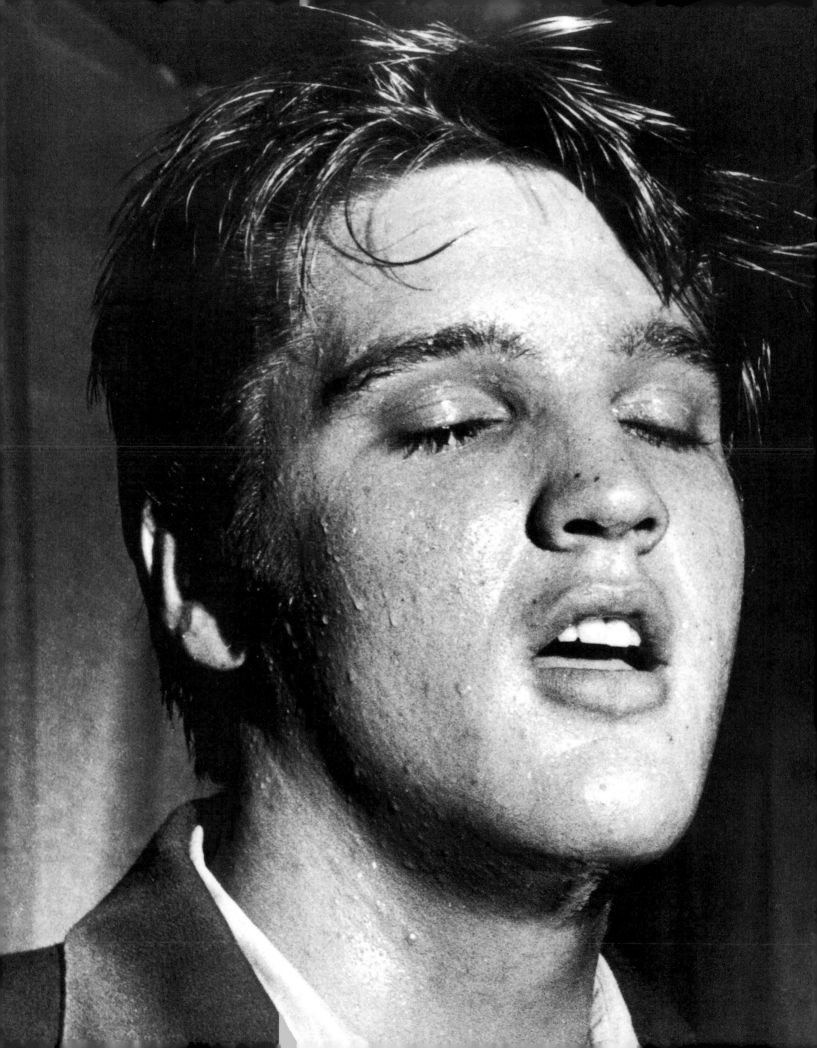

Hail to the King!

★

THE ELVIS PHENOMENON

I t was a sweltering August day in St. Petersburg, Florida, and the 6,500 Elvis Presley
fans who had gathered for that night's two concerts were going a little crazy.
Overcome by excitement, one teenage girl after another burst into happy screams
or tears; six of them fainted. "I can't stand it, I can't stand it," gasped one 15-
year-old to a city patrolman. "I can't stand it either," he replied wearily, "but I'm
not crying about it."

The year was 1956 and across the land Elvis mania was in full swing. Almost unknown outside the South just a year before, the 21-year-old Memphis singer was
suddenly everywhere—performing on television variety shows, topping record charts,
filming his first movie, touring in 25 states. The country had never seen anything like
him. Uninhibited in concert, Elvis moved with barely disguised sexual energy to the new music of rock and roll. His singing was shocking, too, shat-
tering the mold of 1950s pop music with deliberately stuttered words and
unexpected rhythms. With each new hit, the frenzy of the singer's fans
grew; so did the backlash from worried adults. As anyone who was in St.
Petersburg that day would attest, America would never be the same after Elvis Presley.

*Dripping with sweat, Elvis looks exhausted but radiant after an intense 1955 performance (left). By the next
year, his fans were sporting emblems like the button above; from different angles, they could see two images,
either separately or superimposed—a dreamy portrait or a glimpse of Elvis's famous hip-swinging act.*

American Dreamer

Presley said of manager Tom Parker (above, left), "We're the perfect combination. Colonel's an old carny, and me, I'm off the wall."

"I was an overnight sensation. A year after they heard me the first time, they called me back."

Born in a shack on the wrong side of Tupelo, Mississippi, Elvis Presley grew up poor. Yet he never doubted better days lay ahead. "From the time I was a kid I knew something was going to happen to me," he later said. "I didn't know exactly what, but it was a feeling that the future looked kind of bright."

The dream started to become reality in 1953, not long after he graduated from high school in Memphis and went to work at a machinist's shop. As Elvis later told the story, his singing career started by accident. "I went into a record shop to make a record for my mother, just to surprise her," he said. "Some man in there heard me sing and said he might call me some time. He did—more than a year later. He was Sam Phillips, the owner of Sun Records."

In fact, the "record shop" was Phillips's recording studio, and only by dropping by repeatedly did the doggedly hopeful Elvis, now working as a truckdriver, get his attention. On June 26, 1954, Phillips finally had his assistant call Elvis to ask if he could come in. "I was there by the time she hung up the phone," Elvis later joked. The session ended inconclusively, so Phillips tried again on July 5. This time Phillips heard the new sound he was searching for when Elvis let loose with a hillbilly-tinged rendition of a popular rhythm and blues song, "That's All Right." The record was a regional sensation.

The reaction to Elvis attracted the attention of "Colonel" Tom Parker (the military rank was honorary), a former carnival promoter who started making deals for Presley in 1955 and became his sole manager the following year. The Colonel arranged for RCA Records to buy out Presley's Sun contract for the then unheard-of sum of $35,000. It was the beginning of a dream fulfilled, the first of many good deals for Elvis—and for the Colonel.

Gladys and Vernon Presley pose with their much loved only son circa 1938. A twin brother, Jesse Garon, was stillborn.

Just two days after Presley recorded "That's All Right," his first single for Sun Records (above), Memphis disc jockey Dewey Phillips played it on his hugely popular Red Hot and Blue show to overwhelming response, lighting the fuse of Elvis's explosive takeoff.

Colonel Tom Parker and Ed Sullivan, seen above at right, talk business as Elvis fine-tunes his hair style. Under the contract Parker negotiated with Sullivan, Presley was paid the record sum of $50,000 for his three appearances on the hit show.

"When I sing this rock 'n' roll, my eyes won't stay open and my legs won't stand still. I don't care what they say, it ain't nasty."

Ticket to the first Sullivan appearance

Elvis in Your Living Room

Tom Parker lost no time parlaying Presley's fanatical following into a national audience by getting him on television, starting on CBS with the Dorsey Brothers' *Stage Show* in January 1956. The reviews were withering. Presley displayed "the kind of animalism that should be confined to dives and bordellos," wrote one critic. Another described the singer's act as all "grunt and groin." The ratings, however, told a different story. Milton Berle's variety show got some of its best numbers of the season—as well as a storm of angry calls and letters—when Elvis was on.

"He's not my cup of tea," said Ed Sullivan, TV's undisputed ratings leader. Then Sullivan's archrival Steve Allen signed up the hot new act. Hoping to make Elvis more acceptable to a family audience, Allen had him appear in a tuxedo—with blue suede shoes. Soon the curtain pulled back to reveal a basset hound seated on a pedestal, to whom an obviously embarrassed Elvis addressed the song "Hound Dog," turning the dog's head toward him as its attention wandered.

Many Elvis fans were so appalled that he felt compelled to reassure them in a concert a few days later that "those folks in New York are not going to change me none." But the general TV audience loved it. For the first time, Allen beat Ed Sullivan in the ratings. Reversing his decision, Sullivan signed Elvis to three appearances. On September 9, 1956, more than 42 million viewers—82.6 percent of the national television audience—saw his debut. By the third show, Sullivan himself seemed a convert. "I want you to know," he told America, "that this is a real decent, fine boy." He still ordered the cameramen to film Elvis only from the waist up, however, thus protecting the nation's moral fiber from further exposure to the singer's swaying hips.

Elvis struts his stuff during a June 1956 appearance on the Milton Berle Show (right). He ended a blistering version of "Hound Dog" with his trademark half-time finish, a technique that never failed to please.

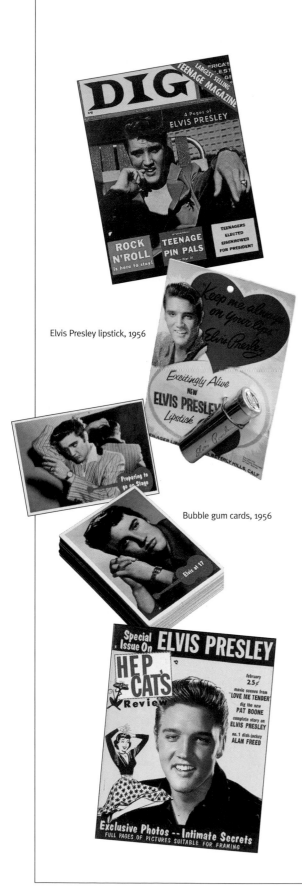

Elvis Presley lipstick, 1956

Bubble gum cards, 1956

50 Million Elvis Fans

Mass hysteria," reported the *Detroit News* of one of Elvis's appearances. Elvis generated the same screaming reaction, especially from his female fans, at every live show. It often got so loud that the band could barely hear their own instruments. After a Jacksonville, Florida, show on May 13, 1955, a mob of girls broke through police lines backstage. Before Elvis got away, they stripped him of his coat, his shirt, and his shoes. Some of his followers obtained his autograph in person *(right),* but most turned to teen magazine articles and to the Elvis merchandise served up by the Colonel. Teddy bears, key rings, jewelry, lipstick (in such colors as "Hound Dog Orange" and "Cruel Red"), and hundreds of other products bearing Presley's image fed teen hunger for a piece of the King.

> "Sure they tear off my clothes, they scratch their initials on my cars, they phone my hotel all night. . . . When they stop, I'll start to worry."

A Presley Hit Parade

Heartbreak Hotel (1956)	That's When Your Heartaches Begin (1957)
I Was the One (1956)	
I Want You, I Need You, I Love You (1956)	Teddy Bear (1957)
	Loving You (1957)
Hound Dog (1956)	Jailhouse Rock (1957)
Don't Be Cruel (1956)	Treat Me Nice (1957)
Love Me Tender (1956)	One Night (1958)
Anyway You Want Me (1956)	A Fool Such As I (1959)
Too Much (1957)	I Need Your Love Tonight (1959)
All Shook Up (1957)	A Big Hunk O' Love (1959)

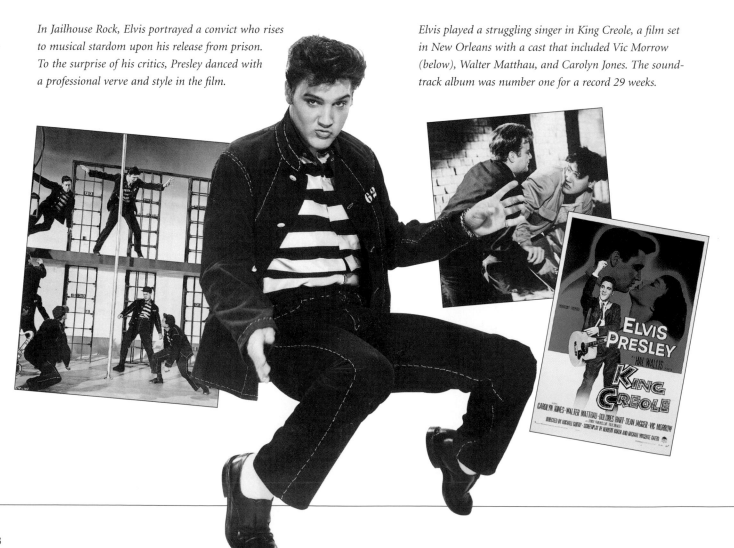

Presley's first foray into Hollywood was for a movie originally entitled The Reno Brothers, costarring Debra Paget (above). The name was changed to Love Me Tender to capitalize on the success of the soundtrack song.

Loving You, Elvis's second movie, costarred Dolores Hart (above); it was the first of several Presley films with a quasi-biographical story line. The singer's parents, Vernon and Gladys, appeared as extras in one of the closing scenes.

In Jailhouse Rock, Elvis portrayed a convict who rises to musical stardom upon his release from prison. To the surprise of his critics, Presley danced with a professional verve and style in the film.

Elvis played a struggling singer in King Creole, a film set in New Orleans with a cast that included Vic Morrow (below), Walter Matthau, and Carolyn Jones. The soundtrack album was number one for a record 29 weeks.

The King Goes to Hollywood

It wasn't long before Hollywood took notice of the seemingly inexhaustible demand for Presley. And to Elvis and Colonel Parker, working in films was the King's next logical career step. "Singers come and go," said Elvis, "but if you're a good actor, you can last a long time." During the late summer and fall of 1956, he made his first movie, *Love Me Tender,* costarring Richard Egan and Debra Paget. In the film, Elvis is on the losing side of a love triangle and dies in the movie's final scene. Girls in theater audiences wept; their jealous dates often cheered. Critics panned the film and were vicious about Presley's acting and singing. "A voice?" asked the reviewer for *Time* magazine. "Or merely a noise, produced like the voice of the cricket, by the violent stridulation of the legs?" But once again, Elvis's fans spoke with a stronger voice: *Love Me Tender* made back its million-dollar cost in less

"I don't know anything about Hollywood, but I know you can't be sexy if you smile. You can't be a rebel if you grin."

than a week and was one of the year's biggest moneymakers.

The next three films Elvis starred in were among the best he ever made. In *Loving You* and *Jailhouse Rock,* he showed improvement as an actor, and at moments the electricity of his charisma came across as powerfully as it did onstage. To Presley himself, the high-water mark of his film career was *King Creole*—"a colorful and lively drama," noted the *New York Times,* "with Elvis Presley doing some surprisingly credible acting."

Elvis signs an autograph during the filming of Loving You. He dyed his hair black for the movie and soon adopted the practice in real life, using Clairol Black Velvet.

Between takes, the King sits pensively in the hot rod from Loving You (above). Overleaf, a gigantic Elvis greets moviegoers at the New York City showing of Love Me Tender.

69

Fruits of Success

When I first knew Elvis," boasted Colonel Tom Parker, "he had a million dollars' worth of talent. Now he has a million dollars." In fact, the total was to amount to more than three million dollars by the end of 1956. At one point he was selling $75,000 worth of

"Everything is going so fine for me that I can't believe it's not a dream. I hope I never wake up."

records a day for RCA and accounted for fully half of its pop music sales. It was almost too much success for the company to keep up with. "We've got Decca and MGM pressing records for us right now because we can't handle it all," said one RCA representative.

To the boy born into abject poverty in Tupelo, the amount of money he was earning seemed unbelievable, even after the Colonel

Below, Elvis shows off the gold lamé suit made for him by Nudie Cohen, tailor to show-business luminaries. At right, he wears black pants with the suit jacket for a performance because, as he discovered, the lamé stuck to his legs when he perspired.

One of the first big gifts Elvis gave his mother was this 1956 Cadillac Fleetwood, which he had custom-painted in her favorite shade of pink. Gladys loved the car, but she never used it herself: She didn't know how to drive.

Elvis, shown in front of Grace-land in 1958, frequently stopped to say hello to the ever present fans at the mansion's gates. "I'd let them all into the house if it were possible," he said, "but there just isn't that much room."

Elvis and his mother and father sing spirituals around the family piano in their home in Memphis. Presley remained extremely close to his parents and bought them everything they had ever dreamed of owning. "We're doing just great," Vernon once confided to a Tupelo friend. "The boy is really taking care of us."

took his 25 percent off the top. Elvis was generous with his money, buying gifts, clothing, luxury cars, and houses for his parents, grandparents, cousins, aunts, uncles, and friends. In 1957 he paid $102,500 for Graceland, a white-columned antebellum-style mansion on the outskirts of Memphis. The living room alone was more than big enough to hold the entire shotgun shack his family was living in when he was born. Elvis decorated his new home with the latest furnishings from department stores in town. Period furniture did not interest the singer at all. "When I was growing up in Tupelo," he remarked with a touch of irony, "I lived with enough antiques to do one for a lifetime."

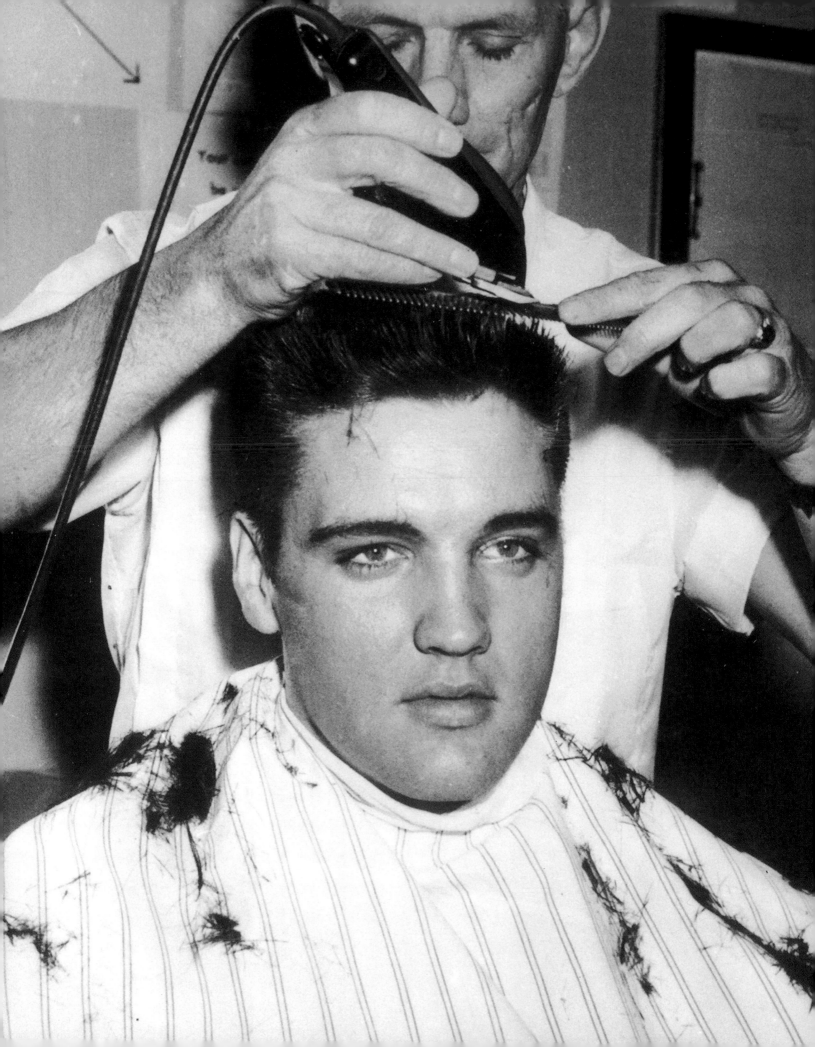

GI Haircuts and Heartbreak

Several hours after Gladys Presley's death, Elvis and Vernon weep inconsolably on the steps of Graceland. "She's all we lived for," Elvis cried. He adored his mother and never ceased grieving for her.

On December 20, 1957, Presley's dream world was rudely invaded by a draft notice from Uncle Sam. Three months later, more than 50 reporters and photographers were on hand to record the historic moment when Elvis got his GI haircut *(left)*. "If I seem nervous," he said, "it's because I am."

The army's most famous private, serial number 53310761, was assigned to the Second Armored Division, the "Hell on Wheels" group made famous by General George Patton during World War II. While stationed at Fort Hood, Texas, for basic training, he got word that his mother had been rushed to the hospital in Memphis. Presley returned home only days before his mother died of complications

"I'll do what I have to—like any American boy."

from hepatitis on August 14, 1958. When her body was laid to rest, Elvis tried to leap into the grave. His depression during the rest of his leave was, said one witness, "the most pitiful sight you ever saw."

But there was little time to grieve. On August 25 he returned to his unit and soon was shipped overseas for a two-year hitch in Germany. The Colonel and RCA marketed records and magazines *(left)* to keep Elvis in the public eye. For the Presleys, the events of the previous 30 months were almost too much to comprehend. As Vernon once asked his only son, "What happened, E? The last thing I remember is I was working in a can factory and you were drivin' a truck."

Priscilla Beaulieu, the 14-year-old stepdaughter of an officer stationed in Germany, waves good-bye to Elvis as he leaves for the United States. The pair began living together after his discharge and married in 1967.

The Teenage American Dream

★

LOOKING INWARD

Middle-class teenagers of the '50s lived in a small, comfortable world whose boundaries were the high school, the movie theater, the football field, and the drive-in. A war might rage in Korea, racial tensions rock the South, and the U.S.S.R. rattle its sword, but typical teens spent little time worrying about such problems. Certainly, the education that high schools were meant to provide was not a top priority. "I guess getting good grades is all right if you do it on the side," a San Francisco high-school girl told a *Look* magazine reporter in 1958. Another graduate once confided, "I used to write notes to my girl-friend in school all the time. We'd meet in the hallway between classes and exchange them. That was the best part about school for me."

According to one survey, teens' greatest concerns were their weight, stage fright, and crushes on the opposite sex—in other words, themselves. In that, the members of the rock and roll gener-ation were not so different from adolescents of other decades. But for the first time, teenagers had the money, the leisure, and the freedom to carve out their own territory in a prosperous and indulgent American society—a place where they could pursue their own youthful, hormonally charged version of the American Dream.

Teen scrapbook

A young man blessed with a strong jaw gets the enthusiastic seal of approval from two Port Jefferson, New York, high-school students. The girl at right wears a flip, a hair style popular in the '50s.

Steady State

I t was supposed to be teen nir-
vana—heading off on a date in
the family car, just the two of
you together for the evening. But
pairing off was not without its anxieties. Boys and girls alike fretted
about not having dates, then fretted
about not knowing what to talk
about when they did have one. And
there were still touchier questions to
wrestle with—kissing on the first
date, necking on the second, deciding
just how far too far to go was. One
11th-grade boy who hadn't mastered
the subtleties of dating or of punctuation declared, "My biggest problem
is Women I can't figure them out."

The solution: going steady. Once
the province of college students, it
was seized on by high-school kids as
a welcome form of social insurance.
Symbolized by the gift of a class
ring, letter sweater, or ID bracelet,
the much coveted state of steadyhood
marked one as simultaneously desir-
able and monogamous.

*Homework, television, and intimacy blend
comfortably for a high-school pair. Going
steady meant being relieved of the burden
of having to make clever conversation.*

Social Animals

When their time was their own, the last thing teen-agers wanted to do was stay home by themselves—and thanks to cars, they didn't have to. Like moths drawn to a flame, they converged on certain soda shops, diners, drive-in restaurants, and other such spots that had, through some mysterious process, become prime teen territory.

Although eating was an essential activity at these gathering places, the quality of the food was definitely secondary. The point was to get together, flirt, size up a potential date, show off, chat, see and be seen. A drugstore counter might serve the purpose, but a drive-in offered an arena far richer in social possibilities. Upon arriving, a carload of friends would cruise slowly around the drive-in to see who was already there, then pull into a space and place their order via a carside intercom or with the carhop who trotted up to the driver's window. For maximum exposure, they piled out to circulate from car to car, shout greetings, hurl insults (generally restricted to males), and bop to the car radio until a carhop emerged with their cheeseburgers and malts.

The parking lot of a suburban Washington, D.C., drive-in doubles as a dance floor (left).

The Costs of Eating Out

A handful of change was all a hungry teen needed at a '50s diner. The typical prices below are from a popular California hangout.

Hamburger	45¢
Hot dog	40¢
Peanut butter sandwich	40¢
Grilled cheese sandwich	40¢
Soup	25¢
Soft drink	10¢
Root beer float	25¢
Milkshake	35¢
Coffee (hot or iced)	10¢
Milk	15¢
Apple pie	30¢
Chocolate cake	20¢
Banana split	60¢

The wall box (below), a remote-selection device connected to a jukebox, was a table-side fixture in diners popular with teens. It cost 10¢ to play one side of a 45-rpm record.

The Rules of Fashion

High-school girls wore uniforms—pretty, colorful, but uniforms nevertheless. For school or a date, nothing would do but a dress or a skirt paired with a neat, close-fitting blouse, sweater, or, even cooler, a sweater set with a string of pearls. Whether pencil slim or outrageously full and rounded out by petticoats, skirts fell well below the knee. A 1957 graduate recalls making her mother "crawl around me with a yardstick measuring my hem. I wouldn't go out of the house in anything that wasn't precisely, exactly 14½ inches from the floor. A quarter inch either way, and I just knew I'd look drippy."

The cool girl wore flats, penny loafers, or well-scuffed saddle shoes with bobbysocks. Local style governed whether to cuff them or not, but one dictum was universal: They had to be white. Colored socks were totally out of it, and so was the hapless wearer.

Dressed in Bermudas and matching blouse, a girl monopolizes the family phone (opposite). Perky and neat, a ponytail (inset) spared a girl the nightly chore of rolling up her hair.

Style Setters

Items like those shown below filled the closets and dresser drawers of girls striving for the feminine, flouncy look. Pullover sweaters were accessorized with detachable collars, and an initial pin individualized a girl's outfit. The poodle was a favorite motif for circle skirts.

Cat's-eye glasses

Basket pocketbook

Charm bracelet

Fur collar

Poodle skirt

Pullover sweater

Saddle shoes

Rolled-up jeans, bobbysocks, and saddle shoes are standard issue for a group of teenage girls.

Crew Cuts and DAs

Fifties cool for boys came in two varieties: clean-cut and greaser. The casual uniform of the clean-cut "Joe College" or "Ivy" crowd called for chinos or khakis with a buckle on the back, button-down shirts, V-neck pullovers or crew-neck Shetland sweaters, and white bucks or penny loafers—preferably Bass Weejuns. To dress up for a dance, a boy might change his chinos for gray flannel trousers and put on a navy blue blazer or tweed jacket and a striped regimental tie.

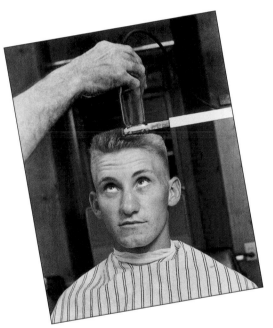

A teenager in Whitewater, Wisconsin, gets a precision flattop haircut from a barber wielding an electric clipper mounted on a swinging arm to keep it level. Hair wax was a boon to boys with fine hair, helping to keep their flattops standing neatly on end.

Butch hair wax

A gaggle of Gary, Indiana, boys projects an air of cool. White socks were the norm for

The greaser look was tougher and flashier, smacking of rebellious behavior if not outright juvenile delinquency. Greasers favored pegged pants or tight black jeans, and they rolled up the sleeves of their T-shirts to show off their biceps and make a handy pocket for stashing a pack of cigarettes. The hallmark greaser hair style was the ducktail, or DA *(right)*. Administrators at one Massachusetts high school were so convinced of the DA's dangerous influence that in 1957 they banned it.

both Joe College types and greasers, although some greasers branched out to pink.

"I just kept [my hat] in my pocket because it messed up my hair."

Ohio teenager, 1959

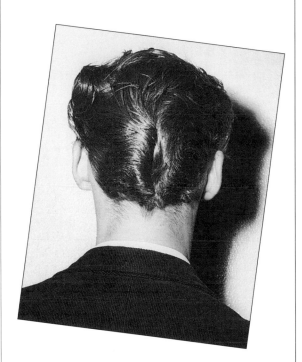

Achieving a well-sculpted ducktail called for Vaseline or heavy doses of such preparations as Wildroot Cream Oil and Brylcreem. A comb was kept at the ready for sweeping stray locks back into position.

Ace pocket comb

A teenage boy and five friends crowd under the hood of his first car, a Mercury, in 1957. Masculine fashion dictated the same casual jacket-and-jeans outfit for every one of them.

Go Team!

With the arrival of fall, boys took to the gridiron to do combat in front of crowds caught in the grip of football mania. The football field was the surest path to athletic glory; not even basketball could equal it. One 1956 high-school graduate, dubbed Crazy Legs for his high-stepping running style, recalls his loss of status when his parents made him quit playing after two years on the football team. He was still a skinny stripling, and they feared beefier players would make hamburger of him. "After that, I was just a regular person again," he says wistfully.

Few varsity sports teams for girls were fielded in the '50s, so they had to make do with reflected glory as cheerleaders or members of the baton twirlers' corps. The girls of the pep club labored out of the spotlight, selling refreshments and planning pep rallies. One such former handmaiden offered a sardonic summary of her high-school sports experience: "We got to put away all the basketballs and gym stuff the boys used, after the games."

Nº 1037

HOMECOMING

HONORING THEODORE and W. McINTYRE

ARMSTRONG HIGH SCHOOL
VS.
PARKER-GRAY H.S.

BROOKS STADIUM

SOUVENIR PROGRAM   10¢   FRIDAY, NOV. 2, 1956

Students from Long Island's Hempstead High School cheer during a football game (above) against archrival Uniondale High in 1958. Led by Captain "Butch" Lopez. the Hempstead 11 triumphed, 36-6.

Letter sweater, Collinsville, Illinois, High School

Football game pennant

The Big Night

The prom was *the* glamour event of the year, when kids shed saddle shoes and jeans for the grown-up allure of white dinner jackets and strapless dresses with floaty skirts of tulle and organza. Unless he was a hopeless turkey, a boy presented his date with a corsage, an item loaded with significance. The prestige flower and the proof of affection was a big purple orchid (never mind that it probably clashed with the girl's dress); daisies could break her heart or send her into a sulk, depending on her feelings about her date.

The dance floor was redolent with perfume—Tabu, Tigress, Evening in Paris—and the scent of pomades like Max Factor's Crewcut, which to one baby boomer was "the prom night equivalent of hot dogs at the ballpark or popcorn at the movies." Good dancers were objects of envy, and for kids with two left feet it was a relief to head out after the band played "Good Night, Ladies."

A gentleman displays his prom-night manners as he helps his date make a graceful exit from the car in June 1953 (right). Later, the couple wear blissful looks during a slow dance in the high-school gym (below).

A girl and her date patiently pose in their 1957 prom finery for the ritual photograph before setting out from her house for the dance. Pearl or rhinestone necklaces, bracelets, and earrings were favorites for formal evenings.

Saved as a memento for decades, this gown was worn by the queen of a Virginia high school's May Dance (right).

Chopstick Swing

Music by
Tech High
Dance Band

Claremont Club
214 Hillcrest
Road

November 29th
1952
8:45 until 11:45

Semi-formal

共
來
作
樂

Promgoers do the bunny hop (left). Dances often had a theme that was carried out in the decorations and invitations (above).

Into the World

Even before high-school seniors got their diplomas, nostalgia could strike, and strike hard. "We all kept talking about graduation so much. I don't know why we'd get so excited, because when it finally came we were feeling terrible," one '50s graduate later recalled. "It felt like I had lost my mother or something, if you can believe that." After graduation, most seniors entered adulthood—a job, the military, marriage; the college bound could keep it at bay a little longer.

At right, seniors at a New York high school try on their graduation caps and gowns. Above is a memory-packed yearbook medley.

Famous Graduates

Every year a new crop of seniors took pride of place in the yearbooks of the '50s, boys in ties and jackets, girls in decorous sweaters and strings of pearls, all poised to march off into the future and make their mark there, whether modest or grand.

Some of the kids who graduated during the decade and made their mark in headline-grabbing ways are shown on these pages as they appeared in their yearbooks, before their names and faces were famous from coast to coast. Morgan Freeman, Raquel Welch, and Shirley MacLaine made it big in Hollywood, Phil Donahue and Charles Kuralt on television. The world of sports was particularly lucky in the great athletes of that vintage who signed on as pros, including Wilt Chamberlain and Jack Nicklaus. Pop music was a major beneficiary of the classes of 1950-1959. Many of the musicians whose work would come to define the '60s—among them Bob Dylan and Paul Simon—actually came of age in the preceding decade.

The hairdos may be fruity and the faces touchingly unlined, but the talent is there, ready to take America by storm.

Johnny Cash, 1950

Quincy Jones, 1950

Carol Burnett, 1951

Sam Donaldson, 1951

Larry King, 1951

Carl Sagan, 1951

Charles Kuralt, 1952

Shirley MacLaine, 1952

Phil Donahue, 1953

Woody Allen, 1953

Morgan Freeman, 1954

Jim Henson, 1954

Johnny Mathis, 1954

Jack Nicholson, 1954

Warren Beatty, 1955

Wilt Chamberlain, 1955

Dustin Hoffman, 1955

Mary Tyler Moore, 1955

Francis Ford Coppola, 1956

Janet Reno, 1956

Jack Nicklaus, 1957

Tom Brokaw, 1958

Faye Dunaway, 1958

Art Garfunkel, 1958

Paul Simon, 1958

Tina Turner, 1958

Raquel Welch, 1958

Ed Bradley, 1959

Bob Dylan, 1959

Jesse Jackson, 1959

Martha Stewart, 1959

Barbra Streisand, 1959

Chasing the Teenage Dollar

★

THE WIDE-OPEN YOUTH MARKET

During the 1950s, American business took note of an amazing development: Teenage consumers were spending more than nine billion dollars a year—about six billion from parental allowances and three billion from their own earnings. And, with few necessities to pay for, the majority of teens were at liberty to buy what they liked. "We just find it neat to spend," admitted one cheerful 15-year-old. "All the teenagers are on that swing."

Not every teen handled money the same way. In 1957, *Life* magazine profiled a 17-year-old who put his $5 weekly allowance into savings bonds, relying on part-time work for spare cash. But *Life* also found another 17-year-old who was probably more typical. Never quite sure where his money went despite a $7 allowance and two jobs, this teen had quite a mystery on his hands. "I can spend the whole weekend doing nothing but watching TV and end up with $5 less in my pocket Sunday night," he told the magazine.

That combination of ample funds and financial inexperience was irresistible to manufacturers and merchants. Teenagers became prime sales targets for everything from skin-cleansing creams *(left),* snack foods, and soft drinks to youth-oriented magazines, movies, and music—including the burgeoning new industry of rock and roll. In 1958, the *New Yorker* magazine summed up the situation: "These days, merchants eye teenagers the way stockmen eye cattle."

In a 1956 magazine advertisement pitching "the friendliest drink on earth" to teenage consumers (right), a straw-crossed couple awash in a bubbly vat of Coca-Cola gaze fondly into one another's eyes.

ARE YOUR PARENTS DELINQUENT?

Take this Behavior Test and see how they rate . . .
This is not a gag or a game, but a Scientifically Exact Test prepared
by the nationally recognized authority, Wells Carr

by Wells Carr

Parent Delinquency Test

WHAT EVERY GIRL SHOULD KNOW

Advice, sports, quizzes, teen idols, and fashion tips were all part of the youth-magazine formula. Most appealing of all, the periodicals wrote about life from the perspective of teenagers—not parents.

Screen Teens

Although she's not king-sized, her finger is ring-sized, Gidget is the girl for me!" So went the opening song of *Gidget (right)*, yet another of a flood of movies made just for America's teenagers. Although they were avid television viewers *(opposite, lower right)*, they were also Hollywood's best customers in the '50s. "Almost any theatre manager will tell you," observed *American Mercury* in 1958, "if it weren't for the teenagers he could close down."

Monsters, hot rods, and rock and roll were favorite subjects of teen features, along with romance, the frothier the better. A few movies, such as *Blue Denim*, tackled serious issues. It was based on a Broadway play about teen pregnancy but had a less controversial outcome than did the play: The heroine decides against abortion. The advertisement for the movie solicited sympathy for her and her boyfriend: "These are no juvenile delinquents. These are nice kids in trouble!"

Faithful beau Moondoggie (James Darren, near right) and the Big Kahuna, a surfer played by Cliff Robertson, vie for the affections of Sandra Dee as Gidget.

Rebels, Beats, and Cool Cats

★

AMERICA'S SHOOK-UP GENERATION

Magazines and television in the '50s consistently portrayed teens as happy-go-lucky and optimistic, their path to the American Dream well marked, straight, and smooth. Those who traveled it were promised security and comfort, and most young people did their best to complete it. But even those who kept their eyes squarely on the road grew restless at times with the journey's blandness. They were also curious about (and sometimes envious of) those who turned off the path—or never started down it in the first place.

America's teenagers might not have joined ranks with the hoods, delinquents, and nonconformists shown on the following pages, but they had fun thinking about them. For many, Holden Caulfield, the free-spirited hero of J. D. Salinger's 1951 bestseller *The Catcher in the Rye,* became a cult figure, as did the real-life beats, whose bohemian lives and supremely cool slang were publicized in the national media.

On-screen rebels like those played by Marlon Brando and James Dean *(right)* were objects of teen fantasy—swooned over by girls who knew that they alone could understand such tortured yet tender souls, and imitated by would-be tough guys. An even safer form of rebellion could be enjoyed in the much loved pages of MAD magazine *(pages 132-135),* which tirelessly punctured the bland platitudes of adult life.

James Dean made young hearts ache in Rebel Without a Cause. "The main thing you felt about him is hurt," said Elia Kazan, the director. "You'd want to put your arm around him and protect him."

The Call of the Wild

The first rebel hero on screen was Marlon Brando's Johnny. The main character of the 1953 movie *The Wild One*, he leads his leather-jacketed motorcycle gang into a peaceful California farm town. The Black Rebels are in an ugly mood because their unruly behavior has just gotten them thrown out of a motorcycle meet in a nearby town. Looking on with approval as his buddies race their Harleys and Triumphs up and down Main Street, Johnny embodied the fantasies of any boy who had ever felt the urge to snarl—as Johnny actually does—"Nobody tells *me* what to do." Yet, like many other '50s screen rebels, he has a tenderer side. When goons from a rival gang threaten Kathie, the daughter of the town policeman, it is he who rescues her. In another scene, the movie also hints at what may have caused him to rebel in the first place: "My father hit harder than that," he sneers after enraged local residents beat him up. Vulnerable, handsome, and virile, able to feel love for Kathie but unable to put it into words, Johnny made many a female moviegoer's heart flutter—and many a date seem like a turkey in comparison.

Although the movie's publicists tried hard to claim it was part of "the national campaign against juvenile delinquency," the film still proved too shocking for many. Fearful that it might incite violence and dismayed by its morally ambiguous ending, in which Johnny and his gang ride off unpunished, a number of cities banned the movie. Brando himself came to consider it a failure. "We started out to do something very worthwhile," he said, "to explain the psychology of the hipster. But . . . instead of finding why young people tend to bunch into groups that seek expression in violence, all that we did was show the violence." Johnny's impact on teenagers, however, was huge, sending sales of motorcycles and leather jackets through the roof.

Marlon Brando as Johnny leans on a bike adorned with a trophy stolen from a legitimate motorcycle club. Black leather was the rebel's symbol.

"Hey, Johnny, what are you rebelling against?"

"Whaddya got?"

Marlon Brando as Johnny

Overleaf: Johnny clashes with Chino, a former member of the Black Rebels who has broken away to lead the rival Beetles Motorcycle Club. Moments later the leaders get into a savage fight, and the two gangs go on a nightlong rampage.

The Eternal Rebel

Americans were just getting to know actor James Dean when he died in a car crash on September 30, 1955, days after completing work on *Giant,* his third major film. His first, *East of Eden,* had premiered earlier that year. His second, *Rebel Without a Cause,* was only days from release. He was 24 years old.

Sullen and edgy, at odds with society's conventions, in love with risk taking, and cursed with what Elia Kazan, the director of *East of Eden,* called "a sense of aloneness and of being persecuted," Dean seemed destined to burn up the trail blazed by his idol, Marlon Brando. His debut in *East of Eden* as the troubled son of a steely California lettuce farmer won him the hearts of teenagers and the raves of critics such as Pauline Kael. "There is a new image in American films," she wrote, "the young boy as beautiful, disturbed animal, so full of love he's defenseless. Maybe the father

Emotionally troubled teenager Jim Stark somberly embraces his girlfriend Judy, played by Natalie Wood, in a scene from Rebel Without a Cause. "All the time I've been looking for someone to love me," she tells him, "and now I love somebody, and it's so easy. Why is it easy now?"

In East of Eden, Dean plays Cal Trask, an insecure loner locked in competition with his twin brother for the love of their stern, devout father, played by Raymond Massey (right).

Kneeling like Mary Magdalene at the foot of the cross, Elizabeth Taylor gazes up at an apparently crucified James Dean in Giant. She, Dean, and Rock Hudson completed work on the film only days before Dean's death. The news so shocked Taylor that she checked into a hospital and remained there for days.

doesn't love him, but the camera does."

Teenage boys adopted him as a "symbol of the fight to make a niche for ourselves in the world of adults" and copied the way he hunched his shoulders, flicked ashes from his cigarettes, and mumbled. Girls dreamed of loving him and soothing his emotional wounds. As one fan put it, Dean was "the embodiment of every romantic idyllic feeling that my body, heart and mind possessed."

Dean liked to tell friends who worried about his daredevil sports-car and motorcycle rides that he wouldn't live past the age of 30, and he boasted more than once that he would live fast, die young, and leave behind a beautiful corpse. But the news of his death still came as a terrific shock. It sent the country into what *Life* magazine called a "movie fan craze for a dead man that surpasses in fervor and morbidity even the hysterical mass mourning that attended the death of Rudolph Valentino in the dim past of the movies."

Thousands of heartbroken fans traveled to Dean's tiny hometown of Fairmount, Indiana, for his funeral on October 9, and more made the trek later to keep the grave piled high with flowers and to chip souvenirs from the tombstone. Hundreds telephoned the studio to beg for the red zippered jacket the actor wore in *Rebel Without a Cause,* and hundreds of thousands stood in line to view Little Bastard, the battered sports car he died in, which was ghoulishly put on display in Los Angeles. Some even paid extra for the eerie thrill of sitting in the driver's seat.

The most compelling testimony to Dean's impact, however, arrived in Hollywood by agency of the postal service—as many as 8,000 letters a month, a fair number of which were addressed not to the studio but to the dead actor himself. Penned by despondent fans who clung to the hope that Dean hadn't been killed at all but was merely keeping a disfigured face from the public eye, many contained pleas for him to come back. "Don't hide, Jimmy," one letter read. "Come back. It won't matter to us."

Most, however, wanted nothing more than a photograph to hang on the bedroom wall or some other memento. "I was wondering," one young mourner wrote pleadingly, "if you would send me a piece of his clothing, just a piece, so I will have something. Even if it's just a piece of his hair when he was small. I don't care what you send just as long as it's something."

The outpouring gave pause even to Hollywood veterans. "He died at just the right time," mused fellow actor Humphrey Bogart. "If he had lived, he'd never have been able to live up to his publicity."

"What better way to die? It's fast and clean and you go out in a blaze of glory."

James Dean on sports-car racing, 1955

Dean's death made front-page news in Los Angeles and across the country. The actor was killed when his Porsche Spyder (below) collided with another automobile on a dusky highway near Paso Robles, California. Forbidden by contract to race while working on Giant, he was driving to a rally scheduled for the weekend after filming ended.

A lonely-looking Dean wanders through Times Square in 1955 (right). One teenage boy wrote after the star's death, "Something in us that is being sat on by convention and held down was, in Dean, free for all the world to see."

Real-Life Rebels

What are we going to do about our young people?" asked Harrison Salisbury, author of the 1958 book *The Shook-Up Generation*. They scoffed at authority. They engaged in antisocial activity. They turned the classroom into a "gang arena" and clogged the youth courts, detention houses, and reformatories. Their conflict with society, Salisbury

---

"What do I want to do in life? Stay alive. Some people say I won't live so long."

A gang member, 1958

---

reported, had grown "deep, relentless and unending."

Those who ran afoul of the law were only a fraction of one percent of the country's adolescent population, sta-

---

The baby-faced leader of a gang revs up his motorcycle as one of his followers falls in behind. "I give my men orders," boasted the tough-talking teen.

tistics showed. And police in New York, Chicago, and Los Angeles considered only one gang in 10 to be violent. But bad conduct by even a small group was grave, Salisbury warned, for delinquency was like a contagion, "capable, at any time, of touching the lives of tens of thousands of youngsters who live in wholesome normal environments."

Such predictions unnerved parents whose children flocked to movies such as *The Wild One,* then adopted the leather jacket, the lingo, and, less often, the attitude of hoods, both real and cinematic. Taking on the trappings of delinquency and actually becoming a delinquent were two different things, as most adults knew. Yet the potential for rebellion was always there, creating an apprehension too great, wrote one magazine, to be "chalked off to the normal crabbiness of elders."

1942 Indian Scout

Hollywood Hoods

Teenage fascination with rebels inspired a new Hollywood genre, the juvenile-delinquency film. The first one released, in 1955, was *Blackboard Jungle,* which starred Glenn Ford *(right)* as an idealistic teacher in a hood-ridden vocational high school. The movie portrayed an America cut cleanly in two—adults on one side, teens on the other. Reviewers, teachers, and parents denounced it, but kids made it a smash hit. Dancing in the aisles as the credits rolled with Bill Haley and His Comets' "Rock Around the Clock" playing full blast, the teens pointed the way to future box-office successes. Subsequent delinquency movies went heavier on the rock and roll and reduced *Blackboard Jungle*'s troubling teen-adult divide to pure cliché, cashing in on teenage enthusiasms without raising parents' hackles.

THE MOST STARTLING PICTURE IN YEARS!

M·G·M's

Blackboard Jungle

Starring

GLENN FORD · ANNE FRANCIS · LOUIS CALHERN

Vic Morrow, Blackboard Jungle's most dangerous delinquent, threatens Sidney Poitier and Glenn Ford. Below, posters advertise similar films, including High School Confidential, with a Jerry Lee Lewis title song.

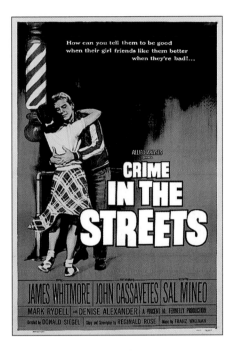

West Side Story

Gang life was elevated to art in *West Side Story,* the 1957 musical retelling of the love story of literature's favorite teens, Romeo and Juliet. Like their Shakespearean models, the star-crossed modern lovers, Tony and Maria, are at odds with their parents and with their society's rules. The musical's gangs, the Jets and the Sharks, stand in for the feuding aristocratic families in *Romeo and Juliet.* Tony is a Jet, and Maria's brother is the leader of the Sharks. The gangs' mutual prejudice and hate inevitably lead to violence *(right)* and to tragedy. But unlike the original, in which both lovers die, only Tony loses his life.

The play ran almost two years on Broadway, but most teens didn't fall for the show's streetwise toughs and doomed lovers until 1961, when the movie version was released. A winner of 10 Academy Awards, it became one of the most popular musical films ever produced.

Bernardo (left), leader of the Sharks, faces off with Riff, his counterpart from the and were so strenuous that during tryouts a doctor was called to nearly every per-

Symbols of teenage passion, Tony and Maria (above) rendezvous secretly on a fire escape. Below, Bernardo's girl, Anita, prances and sings the praises of America in one of the show's liveliest numbers.

Jets, in West Side Story. Dances in the play involved hurling sticks, bricks, and bottles formance to treat injuries. Most of the actors were between the ages of 16 and 23.

William Burroughs

Beat founder William S. Burroughs drew on a 15-year addiction to opium for scenes in his 1959 novel Naked Lunch.

Junk is surrounded by magic and taboos, curses and amulets. I could find my Mexico City connection by radar. "Not this street, the next, right . . . now left. Now right again," and there he is, toothless old woman face and cancelled eyes.

I know this one pusher walks around humming a tune and everybody he passes takes it up. He is so grey and spectral and anonymous they don't see him and think it is their own mind humming the tune. So the customers come in on Smiles, *or* I'm in the Mood for Love, *or* They Say We're Too Young to Go Steady, *or whatever the song is for that day. Sometime you can see maybe fifty ratty-looking junkies squealing sick, running along behind a boy with a harmonica, and there is The Man on a cane seat. . . .*

The Beat Generation

"Any attempt to label an entire generation is unrewarding," wrote novelist John Clellon Holmes in 1952, "and yet the generation which went through the last war, or at least could get a drink easily once it was over, seems to possess a uniform, general quality which demands an adjective."

That generation's members had lived through the losses, the fears, and the dislocations of the war, and they had inherited a peace that, according to Holmes, was "only as secure as the next headline." Their prospects seemed bleak. They might not have to actually make bombs, but it was conceivable that they would be asked to drop some and have a few dropped on them, and this fact never lay far from their minds.

An apt word for such a generation, Holmes wrote, was "beat"—a term coined in the '40s by a circle of misfits in orbit around William S. Burroughs *(left)*, Jack Kerouac, and a young poet by the name of Allen Ginsberg. Implying weariness but also rawness and a feeling of having been used, the term would come to embrace not only the literary movement the group engendered but also the unfettered, moment-to-moment way they lived their lives.

Kerouac became the band's Pied Piper, having given voice to its discontent and restlessness in a 1950 novel in which a young man leaves his family and hometown to seek his true identity in the city. But it was Ginsberg and his poem "Howl" *(right)* that first cast the beats into the nation's spotlight.

He did so at a San Francisco poetry reading held on October 7, 1955, while Burroughs was in the throes of a narcotics addiction and Kerouac was searching for a publisher for his soon-to-be-famous second book, *On the Road.* Fliers for the event promised "sharp new straightforward writing" from Ginsberg and four other unpublished "angels," and about 150 cats and chicks crowded into the Six Gallery, a renovated auto-repair shop, to take it in.

Allen Ginsberg

Ginsberg points to San Francisco's St. Francis Hotel, which inspired some of the imagery in his famous poem.

*I saw the best minds of my generation
destroyed by madness,
starving hysterical naked,
dragging themselves through the negro
streets at dawn looking for
an angry fix,
angelheaded hipsters burning for the ancient heavenly connection
to the starry dynamo in the machinery of night,
who poverty and tatters and hollow-eyed and high sat up smoking
in the supernatural darkness of cold-water flats floating
across the tops of cities contemplating jazz,
who bared their brains to Heaven under the El and saw
Mohammedan angels staggering on tenement roofs
illuminated,
who passed through universities with radiant cool eyes hallucinating
Arkansas and Blake-light tragedy among the scholars of war. . . . .*

"Howl" by Allen Ginsberg

THE POCKET POETS SERIES

HOWL
AND OTHER POEMS
ALLEN GINSBERG
Introduction by
William Carlos Williams

NUMBER FOUR

Customers browse in Lawrence Ferlinghetti's City Lights Bookstore, in San Francisco's North Beach area. A champion of the poetry scene, Ferlinghetti sparked a national debate over obscenity after he published Allen Ginsberg's "Howl," excerpted above.

Cheered on by Kerouac, who prepped the audience with jugs of burgundy and then chanted "Go! Go!" throughout the evening, Ginsberg stole the show. Part rant, part prayer, as much jazz improvisation as barbaric yawp, "Howl" "had an absolutely compelling incantatory quality," as one audience member recalled, "and seemed to be a manifesto for all the misfits of the fifties, the rejected, the deviants, the criminals, and the insane, who could unite under his banner."

Word of the poem spread like wildfire, and Ginsberg was asked to read it many times before larger audiences in the months to come. The hubbub attracted the attention both of Lawrence Ferlinghetti, owner of City Lights Bookstore, who offered to publish the work, and of the local authorities, who considered it obscene. When Ferlinghetti imported an edition of *Howl and Other Poems* that he had published in London late in 1956, they seized it. When he printed another in San Francisco the following year, he was charged with selling lewd and indecent literature and was arrested.

Bay-area bards immediately rallied to Ferlinghetti's side and a prominent lawyer offered to defend him for free, but the drama's most important players turned out to be the national magazines. Their accounts of the trial portrayed Ferlinghetti as a defender of the First Amendment and heralded Ginsberg—called a "wild-eyed shocker" by *Life*—as America's most exciting young poet. The reports helped make *Howl* one of the best-selling books of American poetry ever printed and turned the beat movement into a fad *(pages 130-131)*.

Kerouac's *On the Road*—the Bible of the beat generation—appeared a month after Ferlinghetti was declared innocent. It tells the story of a drifter named Dean Moriarty who turns his back on the squareness and boredom of a steady job and a home in the suburbs to crisscross the continent on devil-may-care jaunts in search of adventure, beauty, and freedom.

Most critics panned the book, likening the cross-country trips to mere adolescent hitchhiking excursions, and Moriarty's reunions with his pals to the mundanity of lodge and business conventions. But even the most dismissive reviewers conceded that Kerouac had successfully got into words whatever it was that was making the nation's "fevered young," as a *Time* reviewer put it, "twitch around the nation's jukeboxes and brawl pointlessly in the midnight streets."

Jack Kerouac

According to beat lore, Jack Kerouac (above) wrote On the Road in an amphetamine-fueled burst in April 1951, hammering out 186,000 words on a single roll of teletype paper 120 yards long. For three weeks he typed away without paragraphing or periods, supplementing the pills with coffee, pea soup, and cigarettes. Once the manuscript was done, even its physical form had meaning for Kerouac, who wrote in a letter to a friend that he had rolled it out on the floor "and it looks like a road." Before that marathon bout of typing, Kerouac had struggled with the novel for two years, repeatedly giving up in frustration. Afterward, he made only relatively modest changes (including the addition of punctuation and paragraph breaks) to what became an American classic soon after its publication in 1957.

a novel
by Jack Kerouac

ON THE ROAD

But then they danced down the streets like dingledodies, and I shambled after as I've been doing all my life after people who interest me, because the only people for me are the mad ones, the ones who are mad to live, mad to talk, mad to be saved, desirous of everything at the same time, the ones who never yawn or say a commonplace thing, but burn, burn, burn like fabulous yellow roman candles exploding like spiders across the stars and in the middle you see the blue centerlight pop and everybody goes "Awww!"

On the Road by Jack Kerouac

Kerouac recites his poetry in a characteristically informal setting in 1959. Eager to move art out of museums, concert halls, and academies, beats gathered for recitations and readings in coffeehouses, nightclubs, and artists' studios like this one.

A Beat Lexicon

Nothing revealed a square in beat's clothing faster than the way he or she talked. Cool cats and chicks spoke the lingo below, which was borrowed from the black vernacular.

Bread: money.

Cat: a man with pizazz; a cool male.

Chick: the female equivalent of "cat."

Cool: composed, indifferent, emotionless ("play it cool"); also a term of approval or admiration ("Cool!").

Crazy: great, interesting, or unusual.

Daddy-O: a term of endearment or respect for a hip male.

Dig: to understand; to pay attention.

Flip: to be either extremely enthusiastic or extremely disturbed by something ("he flipped his wig").

Gas: an exciting event or experience.

Hipster: originally, a drug user who knows how to score drugs; more broadly, someone who is "hip"—in the know or "with it."

Kicks: immediate gratification of desires; also refers to getting drunk or high on drugs.

Later: good-bye; also, "Forget it!"

The Man: a drug pusher; a policeman or narcotics agent.

Nowhere: the opposite of "hip."

Pad: a home or residence.

Put on: to deceive a square.

Square: boring; also, a person who is not "with it."

Turn on: to become interested in something ("she turned me on to beat poetry"); also, to take mind-altering drugs.

Wig: the brain or mind.

From Beat to Beatnik

No expression better summed up America's reaction to the beats than "beatnik," a term first used in print by columnist Herb Caen in 1958. A clever splicing of the words "beat" and "Sputnik"—the name of the beeping Soviet satellite that had sent the country into a panic the year before—"beatnik" made the movement sound un-American and somehow silly to boot.

Jack Kerouac and the other beats hated the term, which caught on quickly. "There are few Americans today," reported *Life* the next year, "to whom the word Beat or the derisive term Beatnik does not conjure up some sort of image—usually a hot-eyed fellow in beard and sandals, or a 'chick' with scraggly hair, long black stockings, heavy eye make-up and an expression which could indicate either hauteur or uneasy digestion."

Entrepreneurs in San Francisco's North Beach area filled buses with tourists willing to pay to see such creatures, and the Vesuvio Café, a longtime beat hangout across the alley from City Lights, did a brisk business selling beatnik kits containing sunglasses, berets, and turtlenecks. "Don't envy Beatniks," read a sign in the café's window, "be one."

Beatnik essentials: jazz album *(inset)* and conga drums

David Amram plays jazz at New York's Five Spot club in 1957. He and Jack Kerouac organized the city's first jazz poetry readings the following year.

Beat poet Diane DePrima, shown with writer LeRoi Jones in New York in 1960, read "Howl" and saw at once "that this Allen Ginsberg, whoever he was, had broken ground for all of us." She and Jones later published a poetry newsletter.

Hollywood Squares

Just two years after the publication of Jack Kerouac's book On the Road had made parents wonder what the world was coming to, the machines of pop culture stripped the beats of their rootlessness, promiscuity, and drug use, transforming them into harmless and sometimes lovable figures. Beatlike characters were written into the radio soap opera Helen Trent and the comic strip "Popeye," and they figured in enough movies, including The Beatniks, Daddy-"O", and The Beat Generation, to enable reviewers to speak of a new genre—the beat-exploitation film. Actor Bob Denver's portrayal of Maynard G. Krebs (above, right) in the television show The Many Loves of Dobie Gillis, on the air from 1959 to 1963, signaled the beats' near total absorption by a culture that had once made them howl.

Rebels With Guffaws

Thirty-two pages long and available for a dime, MAD may have looked like an ordinary comic book when it first landed on the nation's newsstands in 1952 *(left)*. But MAD, as its readers came to know, was like no other publication. Chock full of a one-of-a-kind blend of satire, frammistan, and potrzebie, it marched giddily out of step with all other comic books but matched the gait of America's teenagers stride for stride.

The earliest issues didn't make money. But by the time Superduperman, a send-up of DC Comics' Superman, got his cape in a ruffle for girl reporter Lois Pain in the fourth issue, it was clear MAD had found an audience. Melvin of the Apes—a Tarzan-like creation credited to "Egad (Long-Grain) Rice Burrows"—a deranged Shermlock Shomes, Starchie *(opposite)*, and other parodies followed in subsequent issues, each silli-

"What—me worry?"

Alfred E. Neuman, MAD mascot, 1956

Featured on MAD magazine's cover for the first time, Alfred E. Neuman offers himself as a write-in alternative to official presidential candidates Eisenhower and Stevenson in 1956. "You could do worse," chided the magazine's gaptoothed mascot, "and always have!"

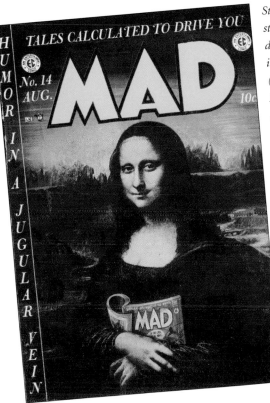

Starchie and Bottleneck substituted for the comic-book duo Archie and Jughead in the June 1954 issue (above), and the Mona Lisa smiled over a copy of MAD in August (left). Other covers proved controversial, including the one at right, from February 1955. Its composition-book look, said one newspaper, made it too easy for kids to sneak MAD into school.

er and more irreverent than the one that preceded it.

Humorless critics of horror and crime comic books threatened to damp the hilarity in 1955, when they forced the industry to adopt a strict code that would censor all comics, including MAD. But publisher William Gaines sidestepped their thrust, relaunching MAD as a magazine. "We really didn't know how MAD, the slick edition, was going to come out," said an artist who worked on the new incarnation. "But the people who were printing it were laughing and getting a big kick out of it, so we said, 'This has got to be good.' "

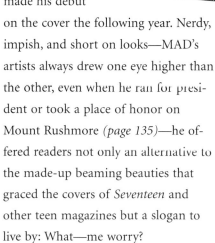

Alfred E. Neuman, the new magazine's jug-eared mascot, made his debut on the cover the following year. Nerdy, impish, and short on looks—MAD's artists always drew one eye higher than the other, even when he ran for president or took a place of honor on Mount Rushmore *(page 135)*—he offered readers not only an alternative to the made-up beaming beauties that graced the covers of *Seventeen* and other teen magazines but a slogan to live by: What—me worry?

Humor in a Jugular Vein

A master purveyor of broad-brush lampoons of Mickey Mouse, Elvis, and other pop culture figures, MAD also regularly hid laughs in the fine print. Arturo Toscanini, for example, teams up with Bill Haley's Comets on a record label at right, and painter Norman Rocknroll is credited with the Crust ad below. The ad carries the Good Housewrecking seal.

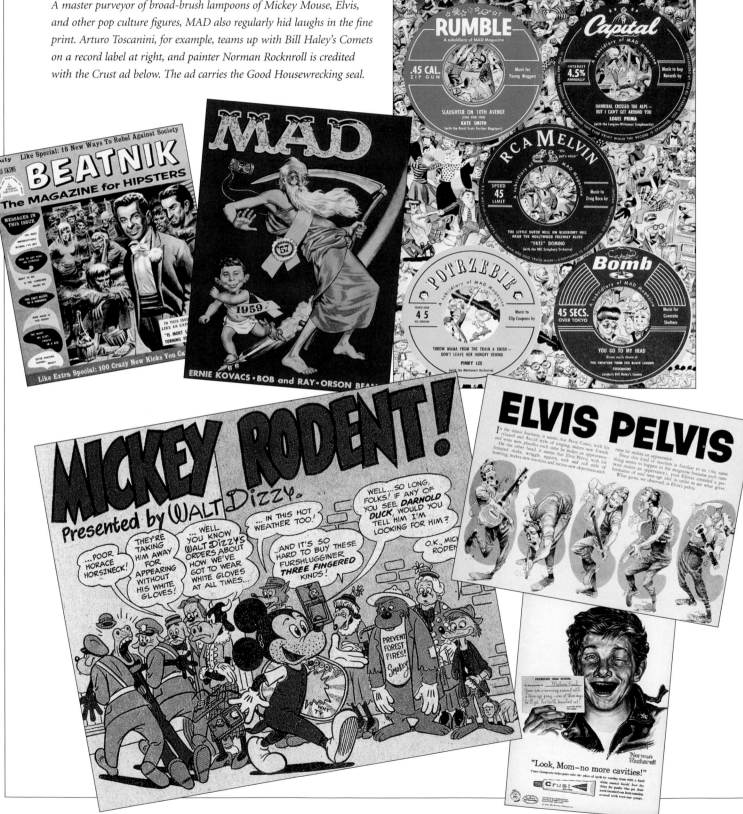

Romancing
the Roadster

★

HOT ROD FEVER

I n all teenage life, there was nothing so cool as a hot rod. A car—any car—gave its
proud owner freedom and social standing, but a hot rod took that to a new level.
The appeal of souped-up, slicked-up cars was all but universal among male teens. Any one
of them with a hormonal itch for speed and self-expression—and a pair of tolerant parents—could find himself a junkyard jalopy to transform into his daily transportation, his
racing chariot, his girl-getting machine. "If you had power-packed dual
exhausts, you gained instant recognition," one youngster later recalled.
"Chicks would flock to you for a ride."

For most enthusiasts, competition was the ultimate expression of hot rod fever. Like hot rods themselves, drag racing went
back for decades in American life, but it reached new heights in
the 1950s. In 1957 *Life* magazine noted that the "drag racing
rage" boasted 100,000 hot rods. Some competed in the growing
number of official races. But any evening this more casual scenario
might be played out: Some 17-year-old would be sitting at a stoplight in his roadster,
engine rumbling like a puma's purr. Another kid would drift up in his machine: "Wanna
drag?" The light turned green—and off they roared.

---

*A paradigm of the era was the Deuce, a 1932 Model B Ford. The one at left has a radically reworked body
and a chromed and blown, or supercharged, V-8 engine. Magazines provided how-to information (inset).*

Two guys apply themselves to their Deuce in front of Dave's Home of Chrome in North Hollywood, California.

Chop and Drop

The challenge was to take a hunk of Detroit metal and turn it into an eye-popper with rubber-burning acceleration. "Change everything" seemed to be the only rule. Evenings and weekends, the car owners and their pals channeled and chopped, raked and dropped, hopped up the engines and chromed their parts. The speed and specialty shops supplied the add-ons, and the proliferating magazines offered all sorts of ideas and know-how. Racing roadsters such as the Deuce turned out spiffy as well as swift, but then in the late 1950s a new craze caught on: the custom car *(pages 144-145)*, often a Mercury coupe, where the chief goal was the artistry itself. As one observer put it, these cars were "the automotive equivalent of expressionism."

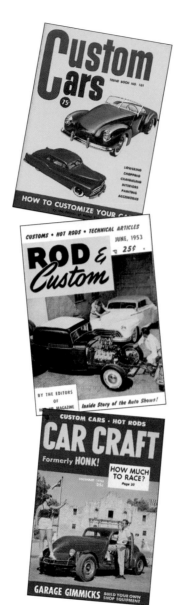

Ford's famed flathead V-8 engine, produced between 1932 and 1953, was cheap, rugged, and easy to supercharge with multicarburetor manifolds and a toolbox full of other tricks. Its factory rating was 85 horsepower, but a hot rodder could put 200 ponies under his hood.

A Glossary of Hot Rod Lingo

A-bomb: a supercharged 1920s-era Model A Ford.

Bent eight: a V-8 engine.

Blower: a supercharger; a blown engine that has been supercharged.

Blow off: to beat your competitor.

Bore: to enlarge the diameter of a cylinder for more power by boring it out. *See* **Stroke.**

Channel: to lower the body by dropping it down over the frame rails.

Chop: to cut out part of a coupe or sedan body to lower the top and reduce wind drag.

Drag race: a quarter-mile acceleration contest between two hot rods from a standing start.

Dragster: a car built for drag racing.

Drop: to lower the body by adjusting the axles, frame, or suspension.

Flathead: an engine with the valves built into the cylinder block instead of the head.

French: to remove the chrome and blend headlights and taillights smoothly into the line of the fender.

Nitro: any of the nitroglycerin compounds added to racing fuel for extra power.

Rake: to tilt the car forward for that mean look by mounting smaller tires in front, bigger tires in back.

Squirt brakes: hydraulic brakes in place of mechanical ones.

Stick a foot in the pot: to floor the accelerator. Also, stand on it.

Stroke: to lengthen the distance the piston travels in the cylinder, thereby increasing its size and ability to deliver power.

Three on the tree: a hot rod's steering-column-mounted stick shift, as opposed to a sports car's "four on the floor."

Hanging Out, Catching Hell

The drive-in burger joint was the hot rodders' clubhouse and Temple, the place where they came to hang out, worship each other's creations, and issue the ritual betcha-I-can-beat-you. Wasn't racing your rod the point of it all, anyway? Sometimes a drag was no more than two guys revving it up at a red light. But often several hundred rodders would turn a section of lightly traveled road into an impromptu drag strip. It was noisy—kids whooping, engines thundering, rock and roll blaring. Dangerous, too. The cops responded with raids that resulted in scores of citations for speeding, driving with inadequate safety equipment, and creating a public nuisance.

Hollywood, of course, went to town on the notion of rod-happy

> ## "Ownership of the 'hot rod' car is presumptive evidence of an intent to speed."
>
> Thomas Ryan, Director, New York Division of Safety

teenage rebels *(right)*. And as the flood of movies heightened concern over soaring accident rates, politicians talked about reining in those crazy delinquents, maybe even outlawing their killer machines. But the hot rodders beat the pols to the punch. They started safety-conscious clubs that made peace with the police and sponsored carefully controlled drag meets. A whole new spectator sport was born.

Norm Grabowsky and pal make the California scene in Grabowsky's $8,000 Ford, complete with full-house Cadillac engine and rear racing slicks.

Drag Heaven

The first truly organized and officially sanctioned drag races came smoking off the line on July 2, 1950, at an airstrip in Santa Ana, California. So popular was the sport that a mere six years later, the National Hot Rod Association (NHRA) counted no fewer than 130 legal drag strips in 40 states with 2,500,000 fans cheering themselves hoarse at all the speed and fun. The rage had come of age.

In most cases, the strips were half-mile-long sections of unused runway, but they didn't have to be; on Long Island, the Glen Cove police obligingly closed off a section of a city street for twice-monthly drag-racing competitions. The souped-up, stripped-down cars blasted off two by two in quarter-mile elimination heats, and the drivers who were able to last through the afternoon earned the title "Top Eliminator" in their class.

Each winner was rewarded with a trophy (17,000 were awarded in 1956)—and a kiss from a pretty girl.

Club plaque for a car

NHRA emblem

A high-flying flagman gives them the green at a 1957 Fort Worth drag. Built for racing only, these dragsters could easily top 100 mph by the end of the quarter mile.

Badges of belonging, these jackets marked their owners as members of a hot rod club.

Swamp Rat, the proud possession of Florida's Don "Big Daddy" Garlits, features a supercharged, nitro-fueled engine that could deliver up to 700 hp and 180 mph for the quarter.

Custom Classics

The custom car was the automotive version of art for art's sake, its lines smooth and flowing, its chrome jewel like, its finish twinkling with five coats of lacquer. Its purpose was simple: to show off its creator's individuality and imagination. The treatments were infinitely varied, but even the wildest flame-licked custom never raced. It just cruised, art in motion.

A candy apple red '52 Mercury convertible with customized Packard taillights.

A yellow 1933 coupe with moon wheel covers and a chopped top.

Tops for its time, a '51 Mercury from Los Angeles's famed Barris Custom Shop.

A '51 Ford with frenched lights, fancy paint, and a Pontiac grille.

Sleek and chopped, a '50 Buick fastback that began as a junkyard hulk.

The X51, a '51 Ford renowned for its wild fins and taillights.

A pink '41 Ford with a chopped top and a fully packed derrière.

Testimony to the flame painter's art on a chopped '50 Mercury coupe.

Frenched lights, rounded bumpers, and a grinning grille on a '51 Ford.

Corvette teeth and a lavender pearl paint job on a '51 Chevy.

Considered tame, a '55 Chevy hardtop dressed up with a molded grille.

ACKNOWLEDGMENTS

The editors wish to thank the following individuals and institutions for their valuable assistance in the preparation of this volume:
Joan Ahearn, Schenectady Museum, Schenectady, N.Y.; Maridah Ahmad, Rock and Roll Hall of Fame and Museum, Cleveland; Richard Allen, Lynden, Wash.; Judy and Ed Ashley, Jed Collectibles, Pemberton, N.J.; Karyn Butler, Elvis Presley Enterprises, Inc., Memphis; Logan Carr, dick clark productions, Burbank, Calif.; Joshua Cox, Museum of Cosmetology Arts and Sciences, St. Louis; Audrey Davis, Alexandria Black History Resource Center, Alexandria, Va.; Mitchell Diamond, Medford, Mass.; Jeff Elmendorf, Funk & Junk, Alexandria, Va.; Sharon Fox, Chicago; Dave Frees, "American Bandstand" Fan Club, Adamstown, Pa.; Pat Ganahl, Glendale, Calif.; Larry Glickman, Publications International Ltd., Lincolnwood, Ill.; Bill Griggs, Rockin' 50s Collection, Lubbock, Tex.; Michael Harris, Alexandria, Va.; James Henke, Rock and Roll Hall of Fame and Museum, Cleveland; Maureen Mata, Pat Boone Enterprises, Inc., Los Angeles; Todd Morgan, Elvis Presley Enterprises, Inc., Memphis; Fran and Gant Redmon, Alexandria, Va.; Harry Rinker, Rinker Enterprises, Emmaus, Pa.; Robin C. Rosaaen, San Jose, Calif.; Val Shively, R&B Records, Upper Darby, Pa.; Milo Stewart Jr., National Baseball Hall of Fame and Museum, Cooperstown, N.Y.; Terry Stewart, Marvel Entertainment Group, Inc., New York; Sara Stone, Episcopal High School, Alexandria, Va.; George Theofiles, "Miscellaneous Man," New Freedom, Pa.; Hank Thompson, Raleigh, N.C.; Steven B. Weiss, Mels drive-in, Los Angeles.

PICTURE CREDITS

Mass.; James Whitmore, *Life* Magazine © Time Inc. **76, 77:** Eve Arnold/Magnum Photos, Inc., New York; private collection. **78, 79:** Carl Iwasaki, *Life* Magazine, © Time Inc. **80, 81:** Hank Walker, *Life* Magazine © Time Inc.; courtesy Benjamin Thoburn. **82:** UPI/Corbis-Bettmann; courtesy Jane Coughran—courtesy Western Costume Company, North Hollywood, Calif.; courtesy Bob Speziale—courtesy Ellen L. Pattisall; courtesy Kim Sands—Jim de Sève, New York; courtesy Western Costume Company, North Hollywood, Calif.; pin courtesy Mr. and Mrs. Gant Redmon, Alexandria, Va.—© Grace Davies/Omni-Photo Communications, Inc. **83:** No credit. **84, 85:** Cornell Capa, *Life* Magazine © Time Inc. **86, 87:** Tom Abercrombie,—courtesy Billy Lomax; Library of Congress, *Look* Magazine Photograph Collection, Neg. No. L9-57-7134-L Fr. #25; © Herb Alden, *The Oregonian*, Portland, Oreg.—private collection. **88, 89:** A. Y. Owen, *Life* Magazine © Time Inc. **90, 91:** Courtesy Alexandria Black History Resource Center, Alexandria, Va.; Gordon Parks, *Life* Magazine © Time Inc. (2)—courtesy Mr. and Mrs. Gant Redmon, Va.—courtesy Episcopal High School, Alexandria, Va. **92:** UPI/Corbis-Bettmann (2)—The Alexandria Black History Resource Center, Alexandria, Va. **93:** Courtesy Suzanne Fowler; pearls courtesy Anne Whittle; gloves courtesy Mr. and Mrs. Gant Redmon, Alexandria Va.; shoes courtesy Western Costume Company, North Hollywood, Calif.; courtesy Lee Fowler Hyer—Cornell Capa, *Life* Magazine © Time Inc.; courtesy Jane Coughran. **94, 95:** Courtesy James and Mary Carey—courtesy Mr. and Mrs. Gant Redmon, Alexandria, Va.; courtesy Mary Ann Warner Putnam—courtesy Shukura Abdullah; courtesy Paul Mathless; Gordon Parks, *Life* Magazine © Time Inc. **96, 97:** Seth Poppel Yearbook Archives, Merrick, N.Y. **98, 99:** Courtesy Patricia McDaniel, Dublin, Ind.; no credit. **100, 101:** Private collection; by permission of BOYS' LIFE, published by the Boy Scouts of America; courtesy Robin C. Rosaaen, San Jose, Calif.—private collection; Library of Congress, copied by Michael Latil; private collection—private collection; courtesy Robin C. Rosaaen, San Jose, Calif.; by permission of BOYS' LIFE, published by the Boy Scouts of America; private collection. **102:** Movie Still Archives, Harrison, Nebr. **103:** The Kobal Collection, New York; Michael Ochs Archives, Venice, Calif.—Movie Still Archives, Harrison, Nebr. (3); Michael Ochs Archives, Venice, Calif. **104, 105:** Courtesy Antonio Alcalá; courtesy Funk & Junk at http://www.funkandjunk.com; Library of Congress, *Look* Magazine Photograph Collection No. L9-56-6797-O Fr. #13; courtesy Mr. and Mrs. Gant Redmon, Alexandria, Va.; courtesy Neil Kagan; courtesy Funk & Junk at http://www.funkandjunk.com. **106:** Library of Congress, copied by Michael Latil. **107:** No credit; Library of Congress, copied by Michael Latil—no credit (2)—Library of Congress, photos by Michael Latil (2); courtesy Museum of Cosmetology Arts and Sciences, St. Louis, Mo. **108:** No credit—courtesy Funk & Junk at http://www.funkandjunk.com. (2)—courtesy Mr. and Mrs. Gant Redmon, Alexandria, Va. (2). **109:** Paul Schutzer, *Life* Magazine © Time Inc. **110, 111:** Courtesy Goodwin House West, Arlington, Va.; Photofest, New York. **112:** Michael Ochs Archives, Venice, Calif. **113:** Hershenson-Allen Archive, West Plains, Mo. **114, 115:** Movie Still Archives, Harrison, Nebr. **116:** Courtesy G. Barris Collection, photo by David Fetherston—Photofest, New York. **117:** Posters courtesy Hershenson-Allen Archive, West Plains, Mo.; photos courtesy Movie Still Archives, Harrison, Nebr. **118:** David Loehr Collection, Fairmount, Ind.; Corbis-Bettmann. **119:** Dennis Stock/Magnum Photos, Inc., New York. **120, 121:** © George Haling Pictures, New York City; Bob Stark, Starklite Cycle, Perris, Calif. photo by Bernard Fallon. **122, 123:** Movie Still Archives, Harrison, Nebr., posters courtesy Hershenson-Allen Archive, West Plains, Mo. (3). **124, 125:** Hershenson-Allen Archive, West Plains, Mo.; Hank Walker, *Life* Magazine © Time Inc. (3). **126:** © Allen Ginsberg, courtesy of Fahey/Klein Gallery, Los Angeles—private collection. **127:** © Harry Redl, West Vancouver, BC, Canada; private collection—Joern Gerdts. **128:** Fred DeWitt for *Time*. **129:** © Fred W. McDarrah, New York; inset courtesy 84 Charing Cross Bookstore, EH?, Munising, Mich. www.84cc.com. **130:** Courtesy Mimi Harrison—Drums Unlimited/Michael Toperzer, College Park, Md. **131:** Burt Glinn/Magnum Photos, Inc., New York; Movie Still Archives, Harrison, Nebr.—© Fred W. McDarrah, New York. **132-135:** Alfred E. Newman, MAD Magazine and all related elements are copyrights and trademarks of E.C. Publications, Inc. All rights reserved. Used by permission. Magazines courtesy Cliff Keirce collection, except "Starchie" p. 133. **136, 137:** Courtesy Larry Hook, photo by Richard Benjamin; photo by Pat Ganahl. **138:** Ralph Crane, *Life* Magazine © Time Inc. **139:** Courtesy Michael Goyda, photos by Allan Holm (3)—photo by Pat Ganahl. **140:** Ralph Crane, *Life* Magazine © Time Inc. **141:** Michael Ochs Archives, Venice, Calif.; Hershenson-Allen Archive, West Plains, Mo. (3). **142, 143:** Courtesy Michael Goyda, photos by Allan Holm (2); A. Y. Owen, *Life* Magazine © Time Inc.; courtesy Michael Goyda, photos by Allan Holm (3)—dragster courtesy Don Garlits' Museum of Drag Racing, Ocala, Fla., photo by John Jernigan. **144:** Photos by Pat Ganahl. **145:** Photo by Pat Ganahl—© Jay Hirsch, Grand View, N.Y. (2)—photos by Pat Ganahl (3).

BIBLIOGRAPHY

BOOKS

Adler, Dennis. *Fifties Flashback: The American Car.* Osceola, Wis.: Motorbooks International, 1996.

Allen, Frederick. *Secret Formula.* New York: HarperBusiness, 1994.

Amburn, Ellis. *Buddy Holly.* New York: St. Martin's Griffin, 1996.

Anastos, Ernie, with Jack Levin. *'Twixt: Teens Yesterday and Today.* New York: Franklin Watts, 1983.

Automobile and Culture. New York: Harry N. Abrams, 1984.

Barris, George, and David Fetherston. *Barris Kustoms of the 1950s.* Osceola, Wis.: Motorbooks International, 1994.

Batchelor, Dean. *The American Hot Rod.* Osceola, Wis.: Motorbooks International, 1995.

Boone, Pat. *'Twixt Twelve and Twenty.* Englewood Cliffs, N.J.: Prentice-Hall, 1958.

Brando, Marlon, with Robert Lindsey. *Brando: Songs My Mother Taught Me.* New York: Random House, 1994.

Breines, Wini. *Young, White, and Miserable.* Boston: Beacon Press, 1992.

Burroughs, William S. *Naked Lunch.* New York: Grove Press, 1959.

Clark, Dick, with Fred Bronson. *Dick Clark's American Bandstand.* New York: HarperCollins, 1997.

Classic Guitars of the '50s. San Francisco: Miller Freeman, 1996.

Crenshaw, Marshall. *Hollywood Rock.* Ed. by Ted Mico. New York: HarperPerennial, 1994.

Dalton, David. *James Dean.* New York: St. Martin's Press, 1984.

Doherty, Thomas. *Teenagers and Teenpics.* Boston: Unwin Hyman, 1988.

The Fifties: Photographs of America. New York: Pantheon Books, 1985.

Foster, Edward Halsey. *Understanding the Beats.* Columbia: University of South Carolina Press, 1992.

Friedenberg, Edgar Z. *The Vanishing Adolescent.* Boston: Beacon Press, 1959.

Ganahl, Pat. *Hot Rods and Cool Customs.* New York: Abbeville Press, 1995.

Garlits, Don, and Brock Yates. *King of the Dragsters: The Story of Big Daddy "Don" Garlits.* Philadelphia: Chilton Book Company, 1970.

Gilbert, Eugene. *Advertising and Marketing to Young People.* Pleasantville, N.Y.: Printers' Ink Books, 1957.

Gilbert, James. *A Cycle of Outrage: America's Reaction to the Juvenile Delinquent in the 1950s.* New York: Oxford University Press, 1986.

Ginsberg, Allen:
  Howl and Other Poems. San Francisco: City Lights Books, 1959.
  Snapshot Poetics. Ed. by Michael Kohler. San Francisco: Chronicle Books, 1993.

Graebner, William. *Coming of Age in Buffalo: Youth and Authority in the Postwar Era.* Philadelphia: Temple University Press, 1990.

Gray, Michael, and Roger Osborne. *The Elvis Atlas: A Journey Through Elvis Presley's America.* New York: Henry Holt, 1996.

Gribin, Anthony J., and Matthew M. Schiff. *Doo-Wop: The Forgotten Third of Rock 'n Roll.* Iola, Wis.: Krause Publications, 1992.

Guralnick, Peter. *Last Train to Memphis.* Boston: Little, Brown, 1994.

Halberstam, David. *The Fifties.* New York: Fawcett Columbine, 1993.

Holley, Val. *James Dean.* New York: St. Martin's Press, 1995.

Horsley, Fred. *The Hot Rod Handbook.* New York: J. Lowell Pratt, 1965.

Jackson, John A. *Big Beat Heat.* New York: Schirmer Books, 1991.

Kasher, Steven. *The Civil Rights Movement.* New York: Abbeville Press, 1996.

Kerouac, Jack. *On the Road.* New York: Penguin Books, 1991.

The King on the Road. Ed. by Mike Evans. New York: St. Martin's Press, 1996.

Kleinfelder, Rita Lang. *When We Were Young: A Baby-Boomer Yearbook.* New York: Prentice Hall General Reference, 1993.

Lewis, Peter. *The Fifties.* New York: J. B. Lippincott, 1978.

MAD About the Fifties. Boston: Little, Brown, 1997.

Manso, Peter. *Brando: The Biography.* New York: Hyperion, 1994.

Marling, Karal Ann. *Graceland: Going Home With Elvis.* Cambridge, Mass.: Harvard University Press, 1996.

Marlon Brando: Portraits and Film Stills, 1946-1995. Ed. by Lothar Schirmer. New York: Stewart, Tabori and Chang, 1996.

Miles, Barry:
  Ginsberg: A Biography. New York: Simon & Schuster, 1989.
  William Burroughs: El Hombre Invisible. New York: Hyperion, 1993.

Miller, Douglas T., and Marion Nowak. *The Fifties: The Way We Really Were.* Garden City, N.Y.: Doubleday, 1977.

Oakley, J. Ronald. *God's Country.* New York: Dembner Books, 1986.

Ochs, Michael. *Rock Archives.* Garden City, N.Y.: Doubleday, 1984.

Palladino, Grace. *Teenagers.* New York: BasicBooks, 1996.

Palmer, Robert. *Rock and Roll.* New York: Harmony Books, 1995.

Pearce, Chris. *The Fifties: A Pictorial Review.* London: Blossom, 1991.

Pendergrast, Mark. *For God, Country, and Coca-Cola.* New York: Charles Scribner's Sons, 1993.

Phillips, Lisa. *Beat Culture and the New America: 1950-1965.* New York: Whitney Museum of American Art, 1995.

Quigley, Martin, Jr., and Richard Gertner. *Films in America: 1929-1969.* New York: Golden Press, 1970.

Rees, Dafydd, and Luke Crampton. *Encyclopedia of Rock Stars.* New York: DK Publishing, 1996.

Reidelbach, Maria. *Completely MAD.* Boston: Little, Brown, 1991.

Remmers, H. H., and D. H. Radler. *The American Teenager.* Indianapolis: Bobbs-Merrill, 1957.

The Rolling Stone Illustrated History of Rock and Roll. Ed. by Anthony DeCurtis and James Henke with Holly George-Warren. New York: Random House, 1992.

Salisbury, Harrison E. *The Shook-Up Generation.* New York: Harper & Brothers, 1958.

Shore, Michael, with Dick Clark. *The History of American Bandstand.* New York: Ballantine Books, 1985.

Southard, Andy, Jr. *Hot Rods of the 1950s.* Osceola, Wis.: Motorbooks International, 1995.

Spoto, Donald. *Rebel.* New York: HarperPaperbacks, 1996.

Teenage New Jersey: 1941-1975. Ed. by Kathryn Grover. Newark: New Jersey Historical Society, 1997.

Thomas, Tony. *The Films of Marlon Brando.* Secaucus, N.J.: Citadel Press, 1973.

Tytell, John. *Naked Angels.* New York: McGraw-Hill, 1976.

Ward, Ed, Geoffrey Stokes, and Ken Tucker. *Rock of Ages: The Rolling Stone History of Rock and Roll.* New York: Rolling Stone Press, 1986.

Watson, Steven. *The Birth of the Beat Generation: Visionaries, Rebels, and Hipsters, 1944-1960.* New York: Pantheon Books, 1995.

Whitburn, Joel:
  Joel Whitburn's Pop Hits 1940-1954. Menomonee Falls, Wis.: Record Research, 1994.
  Joel Whitburn's Top Pop Singles 1955-1993. Menomonee Falls, Wis.: Record Research, 1994.

Witzel, Michael Karl. *The American Drive-In.* Osceola, Wis.: Motorbooks International, 1994.

Zollo, Richard P., and Virginia Sherry Zollo. *Ladies and Gentlemen Always.* Virginia Beach, Va.: Donning, 1994.

PERIODICALS

Ahlbum, Sumner. "Are You Afraid of Your Teenager?" *Cosmopolitan,* November 1957.

Gehman, Richard. "The Nine Billion Dollars in Hot Little Hands." *Cosmopolitan,* November 1957.

Gilmore, Mikal. "Allen Ginsberg, 1926-1997." *Rolling Stone,* May 29, 1997.

Holmes, John Clellon. "This Is the Beat Generation." *New York Times Magazine,* November 16, 1952.

Life, January 1950-December 1959.

Morgan, Thomas B.:
  "The Adult World Is Treading Water." *Look,* July 23, 1957.
  "How American Teen-Agers Live." *Look,* July 23, 1957.

Rooney, Frank. "Cyclists' Raid." *Harper's,* January 1951.

Time, January 1950-December 1959.

OTHER SOURCES

"The Beat Generation." Liner notes of compact disc compilation set. Rhino Records, 1992.

"Hot Rods and Customs: The Men and Machines of California's Car Culture." Show catalog. Oakland: Oakland Museum of California, September 21, 1996-January 5, 1997.

INDEX

TIME® LIFE BOOKS

Time-Life Books is a division of Time Life Inc.

TIME LIFE INC.
PRESIDENT and CEO: George Artandi

TIME-LIFE BOOKS
PRESIDENT: Stephen R. Frary
PUBLISHER/MANAGING EDITOR: Neil Kagan

OUR AMERICAN CENTURY
Rock & Roll Generation: Teen Life in the 50s

EDITORS: Sarah Brash, Loretta Britten
DIRECTOR, NEW PRODUCT DEVELOPMENT:
Elizabeth D. Ward
MARKETING DIRECTORS: Joseph A. Kuna, Pamela R. Farrell

Deputy Editors: Esther Ferington (principal), Roxie France-Nuriddin, Charles J. Hagner, Kristin Hanneman
Marketing Manager: Janine Wilkin
Picture Associate: Anne Whittle
Senior Copyeditor: Anne Farr
Technical Art Specialist: John Drummond
Picture Coordinator: Betty H. Weatherley
Editorial Assistant: Christine Higgins

Design for **Our American Century** by Antonio Alcalá, Studio A, Alexandria, Virginia.

Special Contributors: Robert M. S. Somerville (editing); Ronald H. Bailey, George Daniels, Patricia Daniels, Elizabeth Schleichert, Robert H. Wooldridge Jr. (writing); Yvonne Cooper, Mimi Harrison, Marilyn Murphy Terrell (research); Marti Davila, Richard Friend, Christina Hagopian (design); Susan Nedrow (index).

Correspondents: Maria Vincenza Aloisi (Paris); Christine Hinze (London), Christina Lieberman (New York).

Director of Finance: Christopher Hearing
Directors of Book Production: Marjann Caldwell, Patricia Pascale
Director of Publishing Technology: Betsi McGrath
Director of Photography and Research: John Conrad Weiser
Director of Editorial Administration: Barbara Levitt
Production Manager: Gertraude Schaefer
Quality Assurance Manager: James King
Chief Librarian: Louise D. Forstall

EDITORIAL CONSULTANT
Richard B. Stolley is currently senior editorial adviser at Time Inc. After 19 years at *Life* magazine as a reporter, bureau chief, and assistant managing editor he became the first managing editor of *People* magazine, a position he held with great success for eight years. He then returned to *Life* magazine as managing editor and later served as editorial director for all Time Inc. magazines. In 1997 Stolley received the Henry Johnson Fisher Award for Lifetime Achievement, the magazine industry's highest honor.

Library of Congress Cataloging-in-Publication Data
Rock & roll generation : teen life in the 50s / by the editors of Time-Life Books ; with a foreword by Dick Clark.
p. cm.—(Our American century)
Includes bibliographical references and index.
ISBN 0-7835-5501-6
1. Popular culture—United States—History—20th century.
2. United States—Social life and customs—1945-1970.
3. Rock music—United States—1951-1960—History and criticism.
I. Time-Life Books. II. Series.
E169. 12.R586 1998   97-32609
306' .0973—dc21   CIP

Text Credits:

Page 126: From *Naked Lunch* by William Burroughs. Copyright © 1959 by William Burroughs, used by permission of Grove Atlantic Inc. **Page 127:** First 16 lines from "Howl" from *Collected Poems 1947-1980* by Allen Ginsberg. Copyright © 1955 by Allen Ginsberg. Reprinted by permission of HarperCollins Publishers, Inc. **Page 129:** From *On the Road* by Jack Kerouac. Copyright © 1955, 1957 by Jack Kerouac; renewed © 1983 by Stella Kerouac, renewed © 1985 by Stella Kerouac and Jan Kerouac. Used by permission of Viking Penguin, a division of Penguin Books USA Inc.

Other History Publications:

What Life Was Like
The American Story
Voices of the Civil War
The American Indians
Lost Civilizations
Mysteries of the Unknown
Time Frame
The Civil War
Cultural Atlas

For information on and a full description of any of the Time-Life Books series listed above, please call 1-800-621-7026 or write:

Reader Information
Time-Life Customer Service
P.O. Box C-32068
Richmond, Virginia 23261-2068